OUR GIRLS

The Queen, accompanied by Lady Betty Cuthbert CBE, Chief Woman Fire Officer, inspects Senior Women Officers.

Our Girls

A Story of the Nation's Wartime Firewomen

CYRIL DEMARNE O.B.E.

The Pentland Press
Edinburgh – Cambridge – Durham – USA

© Cyril Demarne, 1995

First published in 1995 by
The Pentland Press Ltd
1 Hutton Close,
South Church
Bishop Auckland
Durham

ISBN 1–85821-315-0

Typeset by Carnegie Publishing,18 Maynard St, Preston
Printed and bound in Great Britain by Bookcraft (Bath) Ltd.

Contents

List of Illustrations

Foreword

THIS book portrays, I believe for the first time, the magnificent achievements of the women in the Fire Service.

It should be realised that before the war the Fire Brigades throughout the country were a male dominated service, with a strict code of duty and discipline. The thought that women would enter this specialised world of firefighting filled the average fireman with dismay.

It was the women's courage under heavy bombing, combined with their ability to take responsibility, to endure endless sleepless nights and above all their cheerfulness in the face of danger which won the men's admiration and respect.

The National Fire Service, unlike other fighting services, was unique inasmuch that the firemen and firewomen were in one service of which they were all equally proud.

I hope this excellent book will be read by those who remember those far off, inspiring days, and also by their descendants, who may for the first time read with admiration of the part their mothers and grandmothers played some fifty years ago.

Lady Betty Cuthbert CBE
Chief Woman Fire Officer, National Fire Service.

Acknowledgements

A word of thanks to all who have helped in the production of this book.

To the Chief Fire Officer, London Fire and Civil Defence Authority, Mr Brian Robinson, who gave permission to print original pictures from the LFB Photographic Library and for authorising me to seek interviews with women firefighters of the London Fire Brigade.

To Lady Betty Cuthbert CBE, Former Chief Woman Fire Officer, National Fire Service, for allowing me to read her *History of the Women's Branch of the Fire Service, 1938–1946*.

To R. A. Haley Esq. QFSM for compiling the names of Fire Service war dead as reproduced on the Fire Service Memorial.

To the Editor of *Women's Weekly*, who printed by appeal to wartime firewomen to send me their stories and to the 300 plus ladies who replied. To all, my grateful thanks.

Cyril Demarne OBE
Hinxworth, Hertfordshire

Introduction

THE title of this book was coined by a grizzled old officer of the Liverpool Fire Brigade, a veteran of many years service in the docks and industrial quarters of the city.

When, in 1938, it was proposed to recruit women into the fire service he was 'dead against', seeing no place for females in the hitherto man's world of the average fire station.

But, came the blitz and firewomen rose to the challenge. They virtually took over control room operations, thus releasing men for firefighting duties. They drove lorries carrying petrol for pumps working at the centre of activities and officers' cars to blazing buildings, often under attack from bombers spraying firefighters with machine gun fire.

When telephone lines were disrupted, firewomen despatch riders maintained lines of communication, carrying vital messages to controls from the fireground. They drove their motorcycles through bomb-cratered and fire-ringed streets as raiders, seeking fresh targets, cruised menacingly overhead. The crews of field telephone units, many of them composed entirely of women, maintained telephone services, specifically in York when the local service was seriously damaged in an air raid. They climbed trees, lamp posts, bridges etc., seeking suitable points from which to suspend their cables. Firewomen cooks, after preparing meals on unfamiliar paraffin stoves when electricity and gas supplies were cut off by bombing, set out at night with canteen vans to bring refreshment to firemen working at the hot-spots.

The tough old warrior, confronted with the magnificent contribution made by firewomen to the war effort, readily changed his mind. He now sang their praises far and wide, missing no opportunity of referring proudly to the deeds of 'Our Girls' on every possible occasion.

This book is a story of British firewomen in World War II. It is an account of some of their experiences during those memorable days and nights of the blitz and of the V1 and V2 terror weapons that followed.

At the peak period, 30,000 whole time and 50,000 part time firewomen were enrolled in the National Fire Service. Twenty-three firewomen died in the course of duty as a result of enemy action. Their names are commemorated in this book and on a panel at the base of the Fire Service Memorial at St Paul's Cathedral, unveiled by Her Majesty Queen Elizabeth the Queen Mother in May 1991.

Some were decorated for deeds of outstanding bravery and exemplary conduct but the majority just soldiered on, quietly performing the support duties without which the fire service could not have functioned as it did.

CHAPTER ONE

'Join the Auxiliary Fire Service'

A T THE TIME when Hitler and his Axis partners, Italy and Japan, were committing the acts of aggression which, inevitably, would lead to World War II, the fire authorities of the United Kingdom, all 1,660 of them, were considering Home Office Circulars dealing with Air Raids Precautions. They ranged from London, with sixty fire stations manned by a full time force of some 2,000 men, to small rural units provided with archaic equipment, some of it horse drawn and relying on a few volunteers to operate it. And they were autonomous, masters in their own area and beholden to no other.

As the continental situation worsened and it became clear that Hitler would resort to force to achieve his ends, the British Government began to prepare for the defence of the country, particularly in the light of the German and Italian air attacks on the Spanish civil population. Accordingly, the Air Raid Precautions Act was introduced on 1 December 1937, authorising the recruitment of an Auxiliary Fire Service.

The first reference to the recruitment of women into the fire service came in a Home Office (Fire Brigades Division) Circular issued in 1937. Then, in February 1938, the London Fire Brigade was instructed to go ahead with arrangements for the enrolment of women on a voluntary unpaid basis, on the understanding that, if war broke out, they would be expected to serve in a whole time capacity.

This enactment resulted in a sense of outrage in some quarters of the regular fire services. Hitherto, fire brigades had been entirely a male preserve; women were positively barred from fire brigade premises. What would become of the service, especially in war time, if women were allowed into watchrooms? The situation did not bear thinking about!

But the vast majority, once they had recovered from the shock of seeing uniformed women working in fire brigade premises, did their utmost to help them to become proficient in their work and to explain to them something of the organisation and past history of what was, to most of the women, a completely strange and perplexing service. The fact that officers and men came to be proud of the women and took trouble, in so many cases, to teach them something of the traditions and intricacies of the fire brigade, contributed greatly to that splendid morale and *esprit de corps* of the women which became one of the most remarkable features of the WAFS.

Experience in the large provincial fire brigades confirmed what was happening in London, the women responding in similar fashion.

The recruitment of women for the AFS varied throughout the country according to the views of the local authority. In Carlisle, for example, no women, whole or part-time, were recruited before the outbreak of war. In Cardiff, no women were enrolled in a whole time, paid capacity until Nationalisation, in 1941. In Luton, 19 women were enrolled for whole time service before September 1939.

In West Ham, as in many other boroughs, women recruits to the Civil Defence Services were sent to local hospitals or to *ad hoc* centres for medical examination based on the Home Office recommendation. In other areas, volunteers were judged as being suitable or otherwise on their appearance of physical fitness!

In March 1938, the London Fire Brigade agreed upon a provisional figure of 3,800 whole time women, made up of 3,000 clerical staff; 500 drivers and 300 watchroom workers. At first, three categories were envisaged but the clerical staff and watchroom workers were

This couple are modelling the Auxiliary Fire Service Uniform in early 1939. The picture was reproduced as a poster and widely used in the recruiting campaign. Opinions among the women varied; some thought the uniform smart; others had different views. The style was changed later in the war. One enormous bone of contention was that firewomen had to provide their own white shirts, ties and stockings and to surrender clothing coupons for other items.

amalgamated within the first few months. Later, it was found necessary to add the categories of despatch riders and cooks. Eventually,
firewomen were employed as switchboard operators, telephonists,
drivers, cooks, hose repairers, tailoresses, despatch riders, members
of field telephone units and mechanics. After three months the
original figure was revised to 5,750 and it was considered that this
figure, in the event of a two shift system being adopted, would have
to be doubled. Women so enrolled would be members of the
Auxiliary Fire Service; would be provided with uniform and be
encouraged to feel as service-minded as possible. It was also decided
that women should be employed at all levels of control with the
exception of the river service.

Having agreed to appoint women officers, great difficulty soon
arose in finding suitable women to fill these posts, mostly due to
the fact that some of the women officers appointed before the war
gained their promotion not so much on their ability to lead and
organise women, but because they had time to spare or were able
to give their services free. Among them, inevitably, were those who
were inclined to regard the service chiefly as a new form of entertainment and these had to be weeded out from the majority who
were prepared to work hard for very little reward.

In April 1938, a well organised publicity campaign was launched
by Mr Herbert Morrison MP, Leader of the London County Council
and Commander A.N.G. Firebrace, Chief Officer, LFB. The appeal
to women to enrol in the AFS met with such an overwhelming
response that it was found necessary to make every London fire
station a recruitment centre.

Gwyneth Birt was employed in the supply department of the London County Council. She was invited to model the newly designed
uniform for firewomen and duly appeared on an unlikely cat-walk at
the Lambeth Headquarters of the London Fire Brigade. The press had
been invited and were present in strength, to see and to photograph

The first uniform designed for Auxiliary Firewomen. This picture was used extensively in the publicity campaign and attracted many women to the Service.

the new uniform. Small vans had been prepared, carrying signboards advertising the Auxiliary Fire Service. Seeing these, the newsreel cameramen wanted pictures of a uniformed firewomen driving a van across the yard. But Gwyneth, at that time, could not drive, and she was wearing the only uniform available! What to do?

Improvisation is a word not unknown in the fire service and, in no time at all, a fireman was produced to sit on the floor of the car at Gwyneth's feet and do the necessary, as Miss Birt posed with hands on steering wheel, smiling alluringly at the cameras. The photographers were satisfied and their pictures appeared next morning in all the 'Dailies' and on the newsreels in the cinemas. Said Gwyneth, 'To this day I don't know how we escaped disaster.'

As early as the spring of 1938, plans were made to equip every auxiliary with a steel helmet and a service respirator. In addition, they were to be issued with a tunic, skirt or trousers, a cap and a pair of shoes; drivers were also issued with a greatcoat. Stockings were not issued but auxiliaries were asked to wear fawn coloured lisle thread stockings.

Quite apart from the fact that firewomen were required to provide not only their stockings but also white shirts and black ties, a matter for serious complaint was that they also had to part with precious clothing coupons for the privilege. Firewoman Doris Smith, who was a Birmingham District Officer's driver related how the women at her station gave up wearing stockings during the summer months, applying a leg make-up and 'drawing black seams for each other down the back of our legs with an eyebrow pencil.' Others found the leg make-up messy and, when it rained, often became streaky. Instead, they bathed their legs with a solution of permanganate of potash as a substitute.

And fawn coloured stockings to be worn with black shoes outraged many. Firewoman Rowberry, of No. 39 Fire Force, Swindon, was moved to protest:

What! me wear fawn stockings with shoes that are black:
I fear that you're sailing upon the wrong tack.
Yes, I'll help man a pump or a watchroom phone,
Or climb a TL, like Garbo, alone.
I'm sure I'd be thrilled up so terribly high,
Near the pilot's and Spitfire's up in the blue sky.
I'll handle a branch and put out the blitz
But that, No! My mum would have forty fits
That her daughter, good breeding and taste did so lack
As to wear light fawn stockings with shoes that are black.

An indispensable item of equipment in the early days of the war was the respirator. It was anticipated that the enemy would resort to the use of a formidable range of war gases of lethal power. Hence, every civilian in the country was provided with a simple gas mask, even infants, who were placed in a gas-proof, sheet rubber pouch with a large visor, with air pumped in by the mother.

As part of my training, I attended lectures and learned of war gases available to the enemy so frightful in their effect that my training sessions with classes of AFS recruits were treated very seriously indeed.

Those who suffered from claustrophobia had a hard time overcoming their fear of being enclosed in a tight fitting rubber face mask, which gave rise to a clammy skin, and with two windows that steamed up within minutes of the respirator being donned.

My seven year old daughter flatly refused to try hers on and there was nothing we could think of to induce her to wear it. Then came a brain wave.

It was pickling time and my wife and I sat down to an onion peeling session. I explained to Josie that we were wearing our respirators to prevent the onions from making our eyes water. So we donned our masks, her five-year-old sister, too, and started peeling. It was not long before she was casting sidelong glances at her respirator, left handy at her side, and we were able to persuade her to try it on. From that time our trouble was over but I am sure that this problem was not ours alone.

All fire service personnel were issued with service respirators. Instructors in my neck of the woods concentrated on their use and care, with not too much time spent on technical detail. I was given a booklet listing half a dozen of the gases most likely to be used; Mustard; Lewisite; Chloracetophenol and others with similarly weird names. We were told how to recognise them; the smell of almonds, geraniums, pear drops and other colourful descriptions of the properties of the various gases. We made the point that all were dangerous and that the service respirator would give protection against all known war gases.

I cited the story of the cockney drill sergeant instructing a squad of new recruits in bayonet drill. 'Nah, when I says fix, yer don't fix; but when I says BAYNIT's, y'whips 'em out and y'wops 'em on!'

'If, in the middle of an air raid,' I continued, 'you hear the warning gas rattles, or someone kicking up a hell of a noise banging on a sheet of corrugated iron or something, you know what to do; y'whips 'em out and y'wops 'em on!'

Firewomen control room personnel found difficulty in telephoning from behind a respirator face mask; this problem was overcome later by the issue of respirators fitted with a telephone jack.

Operational personnel were issued also with gas-proof suits; jacket, trousers and hood made from an 'oil skin' material, to give protection from liquid gases sprayed from above or scattered by bomb blast.

Fortunately for all concerned, the enemy did not resort to gas warfare; he probably realised that we had some pretty awful gases too, and additionally, the prevailing wind was in our favour so that we could retaliate more effectively had he started a gas war.

During the blitz, firemen quickly discovered that gas suits were useful as waterproofs and that the hood not only protected the back of the neck from drifting sparks but also diverted water from the same region. So the gas suits came in useful, after all.

A number of authorities issued 'bluette' overalls to firewomen telephonists and control room staff, but patterns varied from place to place.

Firewoman Peggy Love, a part-time firewoman who joined up

Preparing for the worst. The threat of gas warfare was taken very seriously in the early days of the war. All operational fire service personnel were issued with a suit of anti-gas clothing.
This is Staff Car driver Enid Fordham rigged for a gas attack.

at Eastcote, Middlesex, remarked that the uniform makers seemed to think that if one was fairly rotund, one had to be seven feet tall! 'But I am only 5 ft 1½ ins. When I got my greatcoat it reached the floor and it looked as if I were on wheels as I walked. When I bent or sat down, the double breasted front shot up to my nose and I had to cut some 12 ins off the bottom, which I made into a pair of mitts. But it wasn't a dead loss. After the war, I trimmed the revers, collar and front with a smooth silvery cloth and made a Russian style hat to match, which saved me a lot of clothing coupons.'

Leading Firewoman Ivy Kemp, of No. 3 Regional Headquarters, Nottingham, was quite proud of her uniform, but somewhat taken aback when she heard people in the streets ask, 'What are they; Australians or New Zealanders?'

Firewoman Irene Hollins was kitted out at Burslem, Stoke on Trent. Her issue included a jacket and skirt, a forage cap and a pair of navy blue knickers. These latter garments, known at LTBs—'lastic top and bottoms—came in all sizes. 'I chose the smallest size but found that the legs reached down almost to my ankles. I soon sorted out this problem, cutting them down to make a neat pair of PT shorts, but I was threatened with a disciplinary charge for damaging Government property.'

Firewoman 'Ricky' Hilliker was not issued with blue LTBs, or of any other colour, for that matter. When the firemen at Sitting-bourne put on a public recruitment display, Ricky volunteered to be rescued from the roof of a tall building. A large crowd gathered and cheered as she appeared, slung over the shoulders of a fireman who proceeded to carry her down the escape. He laid her down and commenced artificial respiration. 'The trouble with me,' said Ricky, 'I am very ticklish and immediately he put his hands on my ribs, my legs shot up in the air and a great roar of laughter rose at the sight of my bright red silk knickers. I never lived it down and resolved that, in the most unlikely event of a similar rescue, I would wear slacks. But I marched off to a generous round of applause from the crowd.'

Firewoman Kathy Ochiltree 'wasn't very keen on the baggy gaberdine jackets with the big patch pockets; the ski caps with flaps that could be pulled down and the trousers that went in tight at the ankles; most unglamorous. However, when travelling on the London Underground, my friends and I must have looked attractive to three American soldiers who, after discussing loudly among themselves which service we belonged to, started to chat us up. We pretended we were in the French Foreign Legion, chatting to each other in broken English and schoolgirl French, managed to convince them that we were with the Free French Forces in Dolphin Square. We made an appointment to meet them there next day; I don't know if they turned up; we certainly did not. The conversation caused considerable amusement among other passengers, who did not let on that we were firewomen.'

Up in Dumfries, Firewoman Mary Cornet was given a pencil and pad and told to write down her measurements for uniform. 'When it arrived, I thought it was very smart and did something for a girl. When we were out we attracted many admiring glances. To help me out with my clothing coupons, my mother took a white shirt from my father's wardrobe and cut it down for me.'

One part-time firewoman, whiling away the lonely hours on watch after midnight, composed a little jingle about her uniform. As a part timer, she was not required to surrender clothing coupons which, perhaps, coloured her outlook:

I have a navy uniform; jacket, skirt and coat
A smart white blouse, severe black tie worn throttled round my throat;
A jockey cap all piped in red and worn with bow in front,
I feel I only need a mount to follow the South Notts Hunt!
Instead of which I have to go to my post at the NFS

A model of efficiency in my brand new fancy dress.
Two nights a week—four hours a night—my virtue all ashine
My uniform all spic and span or else a ten bob fine!
Supplies are scarce, the papers say—they'll get e'en less, not bigger
Why squander on the likes of me I really cannot figure,
When all I want from Board of Trade and NFS together
Are coupons for woollies when it's cold and a fig-leaf for sunny
weather!

Those 'clumpy black shoes' came in for wide criticism. 'I thought
they would ruin my feet but they weren't so bad after they had
been broken in,' remarked several correspondents. Jean Savory re-
called that the same shoes were issued to the local women's prison
but had to be withdrawn; the prisoners were using them as weapons
to attack the warders!

But they were found to be vastly superior to high heeled shoes
when it came to squad drill. Very few volunteers enroling in the
AFS could possibly have foreseen that they would find themselves
on a drill ground, engaged in 'square bashing' as part of their training.
But girls all over the country took to it with great enthusiasm and
generally managed to knock spots off the men and teams representing
WRNS, ATS and WAAF whom they met in competition.

The women of the London AFS in the early days were lucky in
the uniform that was issued as it was smart, sensible and quite
distinctive from any other. The blue and red uniform, with its trim
tunic buttoning at the neck, was popular with the women and
became a familiar sight in London streets.

From 1938 to 1940 an auxiliary obtained her uniform by private
purchase, that is, she was issued with a form signed by her woman
officer to take to a specified branch of a well known outfitters to
be measured for her uniform. This system worked well during the
early days of 1938 when the flow of recruits was small but it broke
down later when large numbers were involved. After the outbreak

of war, some recruits were without uniform for many months, a source of great discontent. By the end of 1939 great difficulty was being experienced in obtaining supplies and the Home Office was being pressed, without avail, to provide each auxiliary, men and women, with two uniforms each.

In February 1941 it was found that the method of individual purchase was too slow and cumbersome. Arrangements were made whereby contractors supplied the LCC with uniforms in a range of stock sizes and auxiliaries attended the central clothing store at Shepherdess Walk, Shoreditch, to be kitted out. Unfortunately, this system, too, proved unsatisfactory as there was insufficient staff available to deal with the huge influx of auxiliaries trying on uniforms.

Other regions throughout the country were experiencing similar delays and the problem was eventually overcome in a variety of ways. Most found it convenient to obtain supplies of uniforms direct from contractors in a variety of stock sizes and made their own arrangements for local issue.

The results were mixed. Some women found themselves issued with a well fitting tunic and skirt which needed no attention; others were not so fortunate. Jean Savory observed, 'If you found a uniform to fit, you were deformed!' Majorie Watkins, at Stratford, East London, size 12, was given a tunic and skirt size 16!

Firewoman Watkins' father was the Station Officer at Stratford fire station and Majorie, feeling somewhat privileged, applied for an interview with the Chief Officer to air her grievance.

'Well,' said the Chief. 'What did you want to see me about?'

'It's about my uniform, sir.'

'What's the matter with it?'

'It's miles too big,' replied little Miss Watkins. 'I'm a size 12, this is size 16.'

The Chief eyed her severely. 'You volunteered for National

Service, not to take part in a mannequin parade.' And that was the end of that.

But, like so many others, Margie got to work with scissors and needle and, with a bit of help from mum, shifted buttons and, with a nip here and a tuck there, turned her shroud into a smart uniform. This was her first lesson in improvisation, a word she was to hear at frequent intervals throughout her service career.

As the number of recruits grew, training sessions were organised. It was realised from the start that if women were to be an asset rather than a liability, they must be given some training, however elementary, as soon as possible. In the early days, men instructors were employed in training women. The control room operators

A G.P.O. trained telephonist operating the P.B.X. Board at a London Control.

were the first to be selected and those experienced in the practical use of telephones and the then standard PBX boards were given preference. Volunteers attended on one or two nights per week, to be instructed in the rudiments of watchroom duties. Details of brigade organisation and procedure were introduced and, gradually, the mystique of brigade jargon dissolved as the girls became proficient.

Said Firewoman Watkins, 'We went once a week for training in the evenings after work. We soon discovered that the fire brigade has a language of its own and we were talking about watches, shouts, pumps and pump escapes, TLs, pull the bells down, turn out, hydrants, stand pipe, key and bar, male and female hose couplings. It was not long before I was referring to the floor as the deck and I continually surprised my friends with my newly acquired vocabulary!'

Firewoman Gladys Birchmore enlisted in March 1939. 'I worked at Selfridges and every Friday after work we attended lectures at a house in Baker Street. We made copious notes about ladders, pumps, hose, couplings, goose necks, water pressures etc. I don't think anyone knew what our job would be if war came—we certainly didn't. But on Friday 1 September we reported as usual and were sent home to pack a case; we were firewomen.'

Firewoman Gladys Gunner lived at Edmonton. 'Looking back to 1938 and the Munich Crisis I wanted to help,' she told me. 'The "Join the AFS" posters displayed all over the Borough prompted me to fill in the enrolment form, with not the slightest idea of where the road ahead would lead. At the weekly training night we were not allowed to touch the equipment demonstrated and were told that if an emergency arose, we should be telephonists but were then assured that it would not arise. Out instructor was a man who clearly did not approve of women in the fire service.'

Women drivers were tested by the London Fire Brigade driving examiner for the district before being allowed to drive LFB vehicles. Those who passed were supplied with a map of London on which the fire stations were marked. Drivers were encouraged to improve their topographical knowledge as much as possible, not only by driving but by covering as much of their own districts as they could on foot. In September 1938, an offer was received via the Secretary of the Women's Automobile and Sports Association from the Auto-dromes School of Driving in South Croydon by which women who had passed the LFB driving test could use the school's private training ground for the purpose of practising night driving without lights and several drivers took advantage of this offer. Further instruction for drivers included brigade organisation and communications, fire prevention and the use of fire extinguishers including stirrup pumps. In addition, first aid to the injured and anti-gas lectures were fitted in as convenient.

Firewoman Peggy Love recalls the time spent wearing her service respirator. 'Regulations were that we had to wear them for thirty minutes once a month. My partner Joan and I were on duty in the watchroom when in walked our new (very dishy) divisional officer. Joan reported to him and he sat down to inspect the Occurrence Book. Joan tapped her wrist, dumbly asking me how long we had to go in our respirators and I replied by raising my two fingers the opposite way to the Victory V sign. At that moment the DO looked up and there was a stunned silence, then we all burst out laughing. Joan and I were a couple of gigglers and the sound coming from behind our face masks was hilarious, at least it was from hers and, I guess, it was the same from mine. Our visors steamed up but we were just able to see the DO grinning all over his face, leave the watchroom. Gas mask drill never was the same after that.'

Win Mercer, an experienced driver, was required to pick up a canteen van, a gift from Canadian firemen, from the London Docks. It was an enormous vehicle and when Win's Oi/c saw it, he decided she must take a Heavy Goods Vehicle driving course at Lambeth HQ. Whilst undergoing her test at the end of this course, she was required to drive her aged London fire pump, minus its ladders, along the famous Lambeth Walk. The street width was reduced by the market stalls and, squeezing past one of the stalls the tarpaulin covering caught up on the ladder gantry, dragging it off the stall. Win stopped and ran back to apologise 'and was met with a flow of obscenity from the stallholder such as I had never heard before. But when he saw I was a woman he calmed down and said "Alright, gel. Good luck."'

The training of despatch riders was similar to that of the car drivers in that considerable attention was paid to familiarising the women with the topography of their districts, and beyond. A popular method of achieving this was the employment of firewomen in testing the street fire alarms in the larger brigade area. Volunteer despatch riders were sent to the New Cross Speedway for courses involving not only driving their motor-cycles but also in their mechanical construction.

Firewoman Rose Sennett's first posting was to Hackney Wick bus garage. The girls occupied a small room with a telephone and their dormitory was the top deck of a bus! 'Many's the night,' said Rose, 'that I slept on the top of a No. 6 bus. Our method was to clamber up the stairs and find a bus with loose seats which we lifted out then placed across the gangway to make a bed of sufficient length. One morning the driver took out the bus on its first run with me in my underwear screaming, "I'm here, take me back to the garage," and scrambling into my uniform as fast as I could. Sometimes I slept on a stretcher in a coach that had been converted into an ambulance but I didn't much care for that; passers by in the garage could see into the coach.

'Fortunately, we didn't stay there long but were moved next door into a place that had been a shelter for homeless men, the "Slop House", we called it. The main room was "L" shaped and the larger part was boarded off into a room for the men whilst we girls had

Instruction in cornering: 'Incline the body gently into the turn'.

the smaller room. The whole place looked clean and neat, with the
beds laid out in a row like a hospital ward. To everyone's delight
there was a small chamber pot under each. It was not long before
someone had strung them out across the room, found a few desert
spoons and turned them into a unique musical instrument.'

Steadily, inexorably, the war clouds gathered. Prime Minister
Chamberlain had returned from his meeting with Hitler in Munich,
waving the notorious piece of paper that, said Mr Chamberlain,
meant that war between England and Germany would never again
occur.

After the early surge, recruitment to the AFS, both men and
women, had languished but, ironically, with the return of the Prime

Minister and his avowed faith in Hitler's pledge, recruits again rushed to enrol. Clearly, they did not share the PM's confidence in the integrity of the German Dictator.

Training proceeded apace. Training centres for firewomen were established and women officers appointed to them; these took over the routine training of firewomen. Suitable volunteers were given instruction by the GPO in telephone operations and procedures, and these took on the training of control room telephonists.

Eventually, women were given greater responsibility in station watch rooms; those who had completed a training course stood watch in an operational station, ready to handle any call that might come in. Confidence quickly grew as the women were introduced to the procedure of handling a fire call and hearing the unabridged jargon in full flow.

There has been no opportunity of instructing firewomen on anything other than the broad details of their duties; certainly, an appreciation of the traditions of the service did not appear on the Home Office curriculum. Yet many became aware that they were now members of a service very close to the public, a body to which people turned in times of emergency and who responded promptly when called upon. Thus, an appreciation of the 'best traditions of the service' became a natural instinct, as countless thousands of firewomen demonstrated as the blitz proceeded. They took on any job short of handling hose on the fireground (some did even that) and performed most creditably.

This Pride of Service extended to women in all parts of the country and, later in the war, was acknowledged in a report by the Officer in Charge of the ATS Selection Board, which examined 90 NFS Senior leading firewomen. The NFS Officers were gratified to receive from the ATS Testing officers, a statement that 'the firewomen had, on the whole, a more mature and individual outlook than the average ATS candidate and that they were particularly

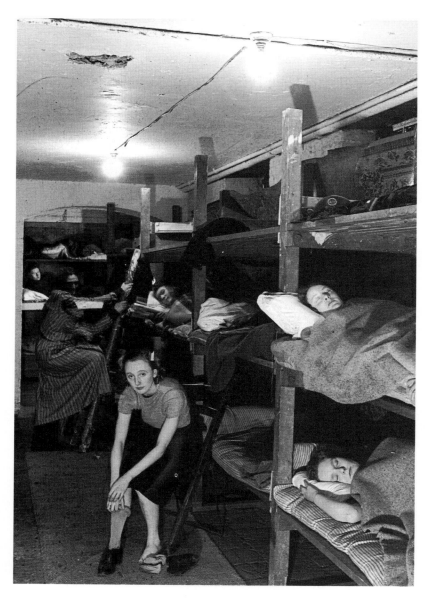

A peep into a typical dormitory built in the basement of a fire station. Timber for the bunks came from bombed buildings. Not exactly palatial, but the girls were grateful for somewhere to lay their weary heads after a long night of heavy bombardment. As Bessie Butler, of Pageant's Wharf, said, 'I fell asleep immediately my head touched the pillow.'

impressed by the general desire shown to put the interests of the
service before any consideration of personal advancement.'

An impromptu skip on the balcony at Clerkenwell fire station.
These girls were early AFS volunteers.

CHAPTER TWO

The Phoney War

THE Auxiliary Fire Service was mobilised on the first of September 1939. Telephone calls were made to those volunteers who had enrolled for whole-time service; thousands of men and women were instructed to report to their local fire stations, taking with them basic rations for forty-eight hours.

A violent thunderstorm broke over London that night, the first night of the blackout. Men and women battled through heavy rain and streets rendered unfamiliar by the intensity of the blackout. They carried kit-bags loaded with food and items of personal equipment, converging on fire stations throughout the capital, guided only by frequent flashes of lightning to light their way. Some arrived bruised and bleeding from collisions with trees, lamp-posts and even other pedestrians.

It would be nice to report that all arrangements for the reception of recruits had been attended to, but that was far from being the case.

Jean Savory booked in to her station, No. 75, Kentish Town. 'I had been measured for uniform a month before,' said Jean, 'but it had not turned up so I, like others reporting to 75, was dressed in civvy clothing.

'We were met by the station officer: "I am glad you've arrived early; there are no women at the City fire stations. You will be attached to No. 68 station, Redcross Street. I have arranged for a taxi to take you there."

'So four of us were bundled into one of the Brigade taxis and off we went to Redcross Street. It was a nightmare journey. The blackout took us by surprise; it was impossible to imagine the effect it would have on travelling. Masks had been fitted to the taxi's headlamps which restricted the light to a dim glow about a yard in front of the vehicle. Other traffic on the roads crawled along; some were fitted with standard masks, others with headlamps daubed with black paint, leaving a circle of about one inch diameter. Out taxi frequently came to a sudden halt when oncoming vehicles strayed from their side of the road. Once we had a narrow escape when a flash of lightning revealed a large lorry bearing down on us from a few yards away. Rain continued to sheet down throughout the journey but, eventually, our driver deposited us safely on the pavement outside Redcross Street station.

'The station officer was informed of our presence.

'"You can't stay here," was his greeting, "we are not having women at City stations, go away." We replied, "Where are we to go?" "Wherever you came from and you can't remain in the station, we are not insured for women." With that, he turned and walked away. But help was at hand in the person of the station's turntable ladder driver, Taffy Davies. He took us up to the fourth floor and found some trestle beds for us. Next day we had another taxi ride, this time to a station designated 68W, opposite Whitbread's Brewery in nearby Chiswell Street.'

This outrageous treatment of volunteers, happily, was not typical. If word had reached the ears of the Chief Officer, that station officer would have been summoned to Headquarters for an interview with Commander Firebrace which would have left him severely deflated, if not a rank lower than when he arrived.

That all LFB officers of the day were not moronic is illustrated in this story and in others to follow:

Whitgift House, a newly erected block of flats in Whitgift Street at the rear of the London Fire Brigade Headquarters, had been taken over by the Fire Service to be used as a hostel for firewomen.

Among those who were accommodated there was a drivers pool consisting of eight firewomen drivers, who were assigned to Room 27. Their duty was to provide transport for officers, among them Arthur Ashton, then station officer at Lambeth. Arthur was popular not only with the men under his command but also with the girls and often was invited up to Room 27 where he regaled the firewomen with tales of his experiences as a fireman and enjoyed a cup of coffee with them.

In 1941, Arthur was promoted to Divisional Officer and transferred to the River Thames Formation. His duty frequently brought him to Lambeth Headquarters when he invariably looked in at Room 27 for a cup of coffee and a chat with whoever happened to be at home. He told the girls of the bitter cold experienced by his crew members when patrolling the river in the depths of winter, whereupon the girls decided to knit woollies for his men. Arthur acknowledged these gifts with a card at Christmas on which he expressed his thanks in rhyme:

> I thank the girls of Room two-seven for woollies sent as gifts from Heaven,
> Which transform cold and dreary nights to passages of warm delights,
> When memory, perforce, runs rife and helps one to forget this strife.
> Again I thank you one and all and hope upon you soon to call, to drink your coffee and hear you say
> 'Oh, Mr Ashton,' in the good old way.

Firewoman Mitzi Spooner remembers being called up at her office and on arriving at her designated station, a school, found only one firewoman sitting in the dark, picking out a tune on the piano by the light of a bicycle lamp, waiting for something, or someone, to turn up!

Margaret Foster reported to LFB A 13 Station, Belsize Park. She was signed on and instructed to report to the factory of Messrs

Lunch time in the women car drivers' pool at Whitgift House, Lambeth.

Manser, Hunt and Cotty. On arrival, Firewoman Foster and her colleagues found the factory, apart from some quite large machinery and a stack of cardboard sheets, absolutely empty. There was no black out, no domestic arrangements, no water, no means of making tea—nothing!

Said Margaret: 'My mother, don't ask me how, got to know that there were no beds available so she dug out a camp bed we had and brought it, complete with pillows and blankets, to our temporary abode. At least I would have a bed to sleep on. As it grew dark we had to grope our way about by the light of torches; we dare not switch the lights on as there were no blackout curtains up at the windows. During the evening I was told to accompany a woman driver on a petrol delivery round. This was the first night of the blackout and she was nervous about going out alone.'

Arriving back after about two hours, Firewoman Foster decided to go to bed but, she related, 'when I reached it there was a very large fireman, fully dressed in firefighting gear, lying on his back and snoring loudly. So what could I do? Here was I, a young girl just nineteen and very shy, confronted by a man in my bed. I slept on the floor.'

Firewoman Dilys Butler was instructed to report to the Chiltonian Biscuit Factory in Lee Green where she was accommodated in the sick bay, taking it in turn with other firewomen to sleep in the only bed-chair available. She gave her rations to the factory canteen staff who cooked her a good breakfast, rather spoilt by the all-pervading, concentrated smell of Lincoln Cream biscuits.

Firewoman Gladys Birchmore was posted to Moon's garage in London's Park Lane where she was directed to the basement. There, she spent the night, trying to sleep on the concrete floor with a single blanket and her suitcase for a pillow! But there was a vast improvement the next morning. She and her companions were billeted in Fountain House Flats, above the garage. After two weeks they were moved to No. 28 Park Street at the rear of the Grosvenor House Hotel where she remained for the next three years. No. 28 was a large house, rather like the TV set for 'Upstairs, Downstairs'; firewomen occupied the attic!'

Said Firewoman Gladys Gunner, '1 September 1939 dawned amid war over Europe and uncertainty over London. AFS personnel were instructed, by telephone and radio, to report to their stations. This highlighted the realisation that one had volunteered, but what for? No one knew. The Local Authorities were as perplexed as the newest recruit that presented herself for duty that night. Conditions at the old Edmonton Fire Station could not have been worse. One room only available, the watchroom with only an outside cold water tap for washing. We were paid £2 a week, our hours 0800 hrs until 2000 hrs seven days a week, worked in two watches. Watches was right; that's all one could do, just watch a phone that never rang; had it done so, the station duty man would never have allowed the telephonists to answer it.

'The night shift was uneventful, except for an occasional "real fire" and the chance to pass with honours at Monopoly! There were no facilities for refreshment; tea was made by the mess manager at his pleasure—so, no tea during the night and the firemen's mess was taboo to the telephonists. A meal, to the value of one shilling, was sent in by the local café and eaten in the watchroom. After some weeks, "Those who Cared" realised that twelve hour shifts in one small room, with no facilities for rest other than the cold, hard floor of the watchroom, would not pay off during the winter. A portion of the appliance room was partitioned off and a small control room was constructed. Telephones were installed, direct lines to sub-stations etc, together with an electric kettle. More telephonists were recruited and we were in business, with the added glamour of light blue "lavy loo" overalls. Still only one outside toilet. Excursions of two or more persons were organised in order that the more nervous types could attend to the needs of nature during the night.'

Firewoman Jessie (Nobby) Clarke was very relieved to reach her station, No. 9 Hammersmith. She had taken her instruction to bring rations very seriously, and had packed her kit-bag with so many tins of food that she was unable to carry it. 'Nobody would help me on or off the trolley bus and I had to drag it along the street,' she related. 'But I was only twenty-two and determination was my companion.'

Iris Greenslade recalls her mobilisation. 'We reported at Lewisham Fire Station, where I had received my preliminary training, on the evening of Friday 1 September, complete with our bags containing a change of clothing and toilet requisites, as instructed. We were ushered into a van and drove through the blackout to our unknown destination. On getting out we saw vague shapes of open sheds and a glimpse of water and were then told we were at Island Yard, our station in the Surrey Commercial Docks. Two days later came the announcement that we were at war with Germany.'

Crayford, Kent firewoman Helen Smith was accommodated in an empty shop with rooms above, close to the fire station. 'Very convenient and near to the Town Hall, where canteen and recreational facilities for Fire and ARP personnel were available,' said Helen. 'Our quarters,' she continued, 'quickly became known to the firemen as The Virgins' Retreat.'

AGO Doris Tyler had reported for duty at her station, Bethnal Green, on the evening before mobilisation day. The whole station complement was busy filling sandbags and the AGO was asked if the firewomen would lend a hand. All volunteered and after about an hour or so of shovelling earth into sacks, was told, 'The Chief Officer is here and wishes to see the woman officer in charge.' Said Doris, 'I wondered what Commander Firebrace would think of a bedraggled, mud-streaked figure in filthy wellingtons but he said, "I have been to a number of stations this evening and this is the first where I have seen the women helping with sand bagging. Please tell them I am very proud of them."'

The London County Council, lacking powers of requisition, had great difficulty in procuring suitable premises for its auxiliary fire stations, particularly in the commercial centres of the capital. Every effort was made to find better quarters, particularly for the women. Gradually, the situation improved and it became possible to remove firewomen from the below standard accommodation they had been forced to occupy in the early days.

West Ham, by comparison, was fortunate. Many of the Borough's school children had been evacuated, leaving a number of schools vacant. These were made available to the fire brigade and it was

Off-duty forewomen relax in their dormitory at Whitgift House, Lambeth.
A carefully posed picture which, nevertheless, portrays the general atmosphere.

possible to provide clean, dry accommodation for both men and women from the time of mobilisation. One drawback was the lack of blackout curtains; this was overcome by painting windows with opaque black paint, which solved the blackout problem but, since windows had to remain shut after blackout time, life was made uncomfortable due to lack of ventilation during those hot, sticky nights of early September 1939.

On Sunday 3 September 1939, Mr Neville Chamberlain came to the microphone and broadcast his message to the Nation.

I am speaking to you from the Cabinet Room at 10 Downing Street. This morning the British Ambassador in Berlin handed the German

Government a final note stating that unless we heard from them by
eleven o'clock that they were prepared at once to withdraw their
troops from Poland, a state of war would exist between us.

I have to tell you now that no such undertaking has been received
and that consequently this country is at war with Germany.

He had hardly finished speaking when the air-raid sirens sounded.
It was no more than was generally expected, an air-raid within
minutes of the Declaration of War and it brought firewomen running
to their action stations. But it turned out to be a false alarm and we
all breathed again, but, from that moment all control rooms were
manned continually.

That night came a further alert. The off duty firewomen at the
'J' District Control at Abbey Road, West Ham, had retired to their
room at the top of the building. Lights had been switched off and
the windows opened to let in air. When the sirens sounded there
was a rush to shut the windows before switching on the lights. In
the confusion, Firewoman Gladys Knibbs had a finger jammed as
the window was slammed shut; she reported to the control room
looking very pale and with one hand held behind her back. I asked
her what was wrong and she replied, 'Oh, it's nothing.' But on
inspection I saw that her finger, wrapped in a blood-stained hand-
kerchief, was badly crushed and she was sent to hospital for treatment.
I was most impressed with her behaviour. The pain must have been
excruciating, as anyone who has smashed a finger will know; but
she was prepared to make light of it and carry on at the switchboard;
an early indication of the fortitude and devotion to duty displayed
by countless firewomen throughout the country when the blitz came.

The London Fire Region Mobilising scheme was brought into
operation. In addition to the LFB Districts—A, B, C, D, E and
F—the sixty-six outer London fire brigades were organised into five
new districts—G, H, J, K and L. The mobilising system was simple;
each brigade was able to use all the available appliances in its area.

The switchboard in London Fire Brigade HQ Control in the early days.
Firewomen were soon to replace the men,
thus releasing them for firefighting duties.

If these proved insufficient to cover all calls, first stage help was called for, to be followed by second and third stage from the District Control, who would order a pre-determined number of appliances from the nearest available source. Should the District run out of reinforcements, it would request the necessary assistance from Regional Fire Control, situated at LFB Headquarters, Lambeth.

Training was resumed with renewed vigour. None knew when the German air attack might come so the rush was on to get recruits through their courses as quickly as possible and posted to stations. Control room staffs initiated mobility exercises which involved pumps reporting to neighbouring fire stations, first within the district then, as experience was gained, to venues farther afield.

Firewoman Iris Greenslade remembers being kept busy 'learning our various duties. We grumbled at times over the repetitive nature of our work but we realised how necessary it had been when the time for action came. But, some months later, it was decided to remove all firewomen from dock stations and I was transferred to Redriffe Road School, still in the dock area.'

Despatch riders learned their way about by delivering messages similarly and the officers' car drivers were employed in delivering stores and light equipment to strategic addresses. As they grew proficient, they were instructed that major roads were impassable, thus requiring drivers to seek alternative routes.

Telephonists and mobilising officers took part in communication exercises. Simulated fire situations involving high fire risk premises were created in which the entire mobilising system was exercised. The aim was to familiarise staff in the operation of the chain of communications; the use of the fire situation boards and the phraseology of ordering appliances to various addresses, plus the system of dealing with calls as they were received. Most of the girls were intelligent and quickly grasped the essentials of the exercises. Those with office experience, typists and book-keepers, were utilised in handling necessary paper work, thus relieving the firemen clerks of their laborious one finger exercises.

Of course, howlers were entered in Occurrence Books. One entry caused a bit of a flap when it was brought to the attention of the Station Officer: 'Tell the oi/c that a Molesting Officers meeting will be held at No. XX station and all available Mobile Officers and Firewomen are to attend.' And another: 'Tell the oi/c that 3 Circular Dames have been erected and are ready for Brigade use.' But the prize for howlers must go to the young firewoman who was given her first lecture on the Carbon tetrachloride extinguisher by Leading Firewoman Rose Sennett at Homerton Fire Station. 'When I came to check the test papers after the lecture,' said Rose, 'this girl had written, "This extinguisher has a six foot nozzle and must never be used in a confinement. It works like a gents." Surely, surely, I didn't tell her THAT?' was Rose's comment.

Gladys Gunner again. 'We graduated in the art of stirring tea with the handle of a toothbrush; leaving enough water in the kettle to boil an egg and to recognise the Chief's footsteps before he reached the door of the control room. To write with nonchalance the words "Omitted to book" in the Occurrence Book and to struggle with one's self-consciousness when first donning uniform; tunic, hat, slacks, tie and worst of all, tying the tie!'

Firewomen Nan Oliver and her friend Mary Shaw had enlisted in Nottingham. They were posted to Fire Control at Benwell Towers, locally reputed to be haunted by the ghost of The Grey Lady. 'The back drive where we entered the war time station was very spooky,' said Nan. 'It was winter, cold and dark and no light to show us the way. We summoned up our courage and walked a few yards into the gloom when an owl suddenly hooted in a nearby tree. We retreated at full speed, tangling our bright, new uniforms in the bushes, where we tugged and pulled to free ourselves. Panic stations. We had to report for duty somehow so we tried again, only to see a faint light illuminating the woods ahead. The Grey Lady! Much to our relief it was a DR pushing his motor bike towards us. He kindly turned around and showed us the way to the watch room entrance. And so we reported for duty; two firewomen, scared stiff and looking as though we had come through a hedge backwards, as indeed we had.'

Down in South Glamorgan, Firewoman Linda Mills was stationed at the Aberkenfig fire station, between Swansea and Barry. Linda's husband wrote to say he would be home on leave from the Army and she applied for leave to coincide with his. Her application was turned down, but Linda's priorities differed from those of her seniors; she took french leave!

When she returned, said Linda 'I was hauled up in front of the Chief Officer who gave me a stern lecture on my responsibilities, at the conclusion of which he asked:

'"So what will you do next time your husband has leave?"

'"I shall take time off, sir."

'I think my reply was not entirely unexpected for, with a wide grin on his face and a sideways jerk of his head, he said, "Get out"'

Although, of course, we were unaware of the fact, the 'phoney war' period was upon us. None knew that there was to be a long period free of enemy activity. It was expected that armadas of German bombers would appear over our towns and cities and that we should be subjected to day and night bombing. An official estimate put the number of casualties to be expected at over 500,000 in the first few weeks of the war but this proved to be vastly greater than actually occurred. Large numbers of papier-mâché coffins were supplied to authorities in the target areas in order that they might cope with casualties on the scale expected. The training of AFS personnel was intensified. Firemen were busy practising all aspects of their work; pumps, hose laying, ladder work, relaying water over long distances, topography, rescue work and they were kept busy from early morning until dusk. Firewomen in control rooms initiated communications and mobility exercises and became efficient in the general mobilising of fire appliances and the use of fire situation boards.

The cooks were practising their skills from the word go. Not all of those recruited had had training in cookery. Many were housewives and had learned cooking from their mothers. Firewoman Lillian Somers said, 'Our food at Esher was really good except that one of our civilian kitchen helpers must have had poor eyesight for we often found caterpillars in our greens. The crews complained about her vegetable preparation and she complained about our moaning. Eventually, I gave up eating greens at Esher.'

Firewoman Kathleen Cracknell's memory of the food was, 'that it was pretty grim. The sausages had hardly any meat but plenty of bread; we called them breadcrumbs in battledress. I was rather keen on the "yellow peril", dried egg. It made good omelettes but was no good for cakes. I made some once and when I went down into the canteen for tea, I found the firemen bowling them to one another across the floor.'

'Sometimes we had a duff cook, usually a relief,' said Firewoman Joan Jones. 'We had the Croydon Ambulances at our station and when she appeared, we sent an ambulance out to buy fish and chips and booked it "Ambulance not required" on its return.'

Lilian Hulm joined up in the summer of 1940. After training she was posted to the old No. 61 station, Dockhead (now 'Blackwall' in the TV series *London's Burning*). Said Lilian, 'I acquired five women colleagues and seventy men and so began a new extension to my life. I started by learning a new language, the fire brigade lingo. My boys knew all the tricks and managed to "win" all kinds of stock on the black market. I was never short of stockings, cosmetics or underwear; things just appeared in my kit-bag. The boys taught us how to play snooker, dominoes, darts and all kinds of card games; in return, I was kept busy sewing on badges and buttons; we were just a large family.

'I remember an attack of bronchitis. I reported for sick parade and attended hospital where I was examined and given a large jar of cod liver oil and malt, which I simply hated! If I had been left to my own devices I would have thrown it away, but I reckoned without the boys. I was allowed to eat my dinner but then, out came the cod liver oil and they all stood around watching while I was made to eat a large spoonful. After that, I was given my pudding.'

When Firewoman Dilys Butler was transferred to Lee Green fire station, the women were accommodated on the top floor. Said Dilys, 'We catered for ourselves, taking it in turn to cook, the highlights being baked rabbit and sprats fried in salt. Our station officer fancied himself as a cook and baked us rock cakes to eat in the wee hours.'

Firewoman Win Hunt was busy at the switchboard at 20Y station, West Hampstead, when she received a message calling for volunteer despatch riders. 'I had never been on a motor bike,' said Win, 'but I could ride a bike and decided to put my name forward. They all laughed at me since I am only 5 ft tall. I was sent to the clothing store to be kitted out for my DRs uniform but they only had men's trousers, so, the weekend before I started, my mother cut pieces off the bottoms of the legs and sewed up the flies.

'She then cut off the large V shaped piece at the back where the braces go so that they were not too tight under my armpits. I reported for training at the New Cross Speedway where for three weeks I was taught how to master my heavy motor bike. There were six firewomen and six WRNS on the course and I was one of the two firewomen to pass. It was a pleasant surprise when I was handed a set of WRNS DR's breeches and leather leggings which the Navy donated for every WRNS DR trained. I wore these throughout the war and handed them in when I was demobbed in 1945.

'Despite my stature, I was often taken for a man when in uniform and called upon to help carry casualties. On one occasion I was asked to help a woman down from a tree in her garden. She had been in bed when a V1 exploded nearby and blew her mattress through the walls of her house. She was uninjured.'

AGO Dorothy Whiting remembers the first wartime Christmas at Brighton Control. 'There were several firewomen on duty,' said Dorothy, 'but the civilian staff had gone home leaving a box containing a loaf of bread, margarine and some cheese for our Christmas dinner! We invented toasted cheese sandwiches and were settling down to make the best of it when a kindly neighbour rang and asked if we could spare four firewomen to go and have a meal with them, so at least some of us had some Christmas cheer. The rest ate their sandwiches, listened to the King's Speech and then solemnly stood and toasted him in canteen coffee.'

It is many years since William Shakespeare wrote, 'A little fire is quickly trodden out which, being suffered, rivers cannot quench'; a truism embedded firmly into the mind of every fire brigade recruit by drill class instructors. It is a fact that the first five minutes in the life of a fire are crucial. Leave it to burn and there is no telling when it will end; tackle it in its early stages and it may easily be 'trodden out'.

It is for this reason that much ingenuity has been brought to bear on the subject of assisting fire crews to arrive at the scene of a fire in the shortest possible time after being called. As early as the year 1880, fire alarm posts were erected in London streets to facilitate calling the brigade to an outbreak. Sliding poles installed between floors in fire stations save crews a few valuable seconds in reaching the appliance room. Lights are switched on automatically after dark to light their way when the alarm bells are sounded. Fire station doors fly open when a lanyard is pulled as an appliance moves off; all designed to save a few precious seconds.

In the early days of horse-drawn steam fire engines, crews cleared a way through traffic by shouting, 'Hi-hi-hi', but increasing traffic noises prevented other drivers from hearing the shouts. Accordingly, loud sounding brass bells were fitted to help clear a way for speeding fire appliances, a system adopted for the new motorised fire appliances as they were commissioned. Fortuitously, the distinctive sound of a fire bell signalled a note of assurance to people trapped on upper floors and, perhaps, contemplating jumping, that help was on the way.

I had a striking experience of this in 1946 when attending a call in the early hours to a house well alight in Royal Hospital Road, Chelsea. A solicitor and his wife had been aroused from sleep by fire roaring up the staircase, smoke jetting through the key-hole and paint on the door blistering. Their shouts for help from the window were heard by a passerby who called the firemen; literally, they picked them from their second floor bedroom window-sill and carried them down the escape ladder to safety. Later, a very grateful gentleman told me, 'Never, in my whole lifetime, did I hear such beautiful music as that fire bell approaching.'

In the sixties, the two-tone horn was adopted for use on London Fire Brigade appliances, later to be replaced by sirens emitting penetrating wails and whoops. But any technical advancement, however effective, is of little use if personnel do not take full advantage. The fire service places great reliance on its routine regulations and generations of firefighters have been subjected to the turn-out drill to keep them on their toes.

Brigade Orders required station officers to turn out their crews for drill during each watch to ensure that there is no delay in responding to the call. Woe betide any man who arrived in the appliance room just in time to see his machine disappearing through the doors. The driver would not wait for the late-comer who, inevitably, would find himself on a 'fizzer'—a disciplinary charge. But 'missing' an appliance was relatively rare; when it occurred, it was regarded as a serious offence.

Firewoman Bessie Barrett was a driver/watch room attendant attached to Pageant's Wharf fire station in Rotherhithe. It was part of her duty to drive the station officer's official car for journeys around the area, which included visits to the five auxiliary fire stations for which he was responsible. It was during the 'phoney war' period, before Goering's *Luftwaffe* had set out to raze London to the ground; the auxiliary stations, so far, had experienced very few disturbed nights.

It was around midnight when Station Officer 'Gerry' Knight rang for his driver.

'Come on, Barrett, let's have a bit o' fun. We'll turn the stations out for drill.'

'I wondered what he meant—"a bit o' fun"'—said Bessie, 'but I soon found out.

'We pulled up short of the station and walked along to the entrance, making for the watch room. The station officer gave a sharp ring on the alarm bell mounted by the door; I watched the station spring to life. The watch room attendant was yelling "station officers drill" at the top of her voice; a stream of firemen, pulling their braces over their shoulders, came running from their dormitory area, a few very confused looking firewomen among them. Other firewomen, with hair crimped up in curlers and scrambling into their jackets, came hurrying from their quarters across the passage.

'It was hilarious. I could not begin to describe their expressions as they saw Station Officer Knight, granite faced, standing there. I suppose the sight of me, standing in the background with my hand over my face to hide my mirth, was a further source of embarrassment to some of them. Those who had been out of bounds dashed to collect their tunics whilst the men clambered aboard their appliances and drove into the darkened streets.

'After a few minutes, the sub-officer and leading firemen, now dressed in full fire-fighting gear, ran in to report to the station officer. "Call the Roll," he ordered as the crews lined up and the firewomen, now also correctly dressed, fell in by the watch room, answering their names as they were called. "All present and correct, sir," reported the sub as the station officer began pacing slowly along the ranks, peering closely into each man's face as he passed.

'"I think it is only fair to warn you," he said, addressing the parade, "that I shall be round again to turn you out for drill. Next time I expect to find all hands in their respective quarters." Turning to the sub-officer he snapped, "In the office."

'They emerged a few minutes later, the sub looking distinctly mortified. When Gerrie Knight "tore a strip" he left the patient in need of plastic surgery.

'Back in the car,' said Firewoman Barrett, 'the station officer just said "home". I had enjoyed my first experience of a surprise turn-out drill in the middle of the night and was looking forward to others. I asked if we were not going on to the other stations.

'"No need," he said. "That's put the cat among the pigeons, all right; the buzz'll soon get round and they'll all be expecting a visit from now on."

'I must say I felt a little disappointed,' said Bessie. 'But I was looking forward with relish to relating the story of the night's events to the girls in my dormitory, next morning.'

Jean Stothard was attached to Bishopsgate fire station, a Victorian edifice with rather cramped domestic quarters. There was no room for dormitories for firewomen in the station but accommodation was found for them in nearby Houndsditch. Jean and her colleagues were intrigued by the nightly ritual followed by one of the girls, an attractive brunette.

Said Jean, 'It was the same performance every night. Before retiring, she got out her make-up box and set to work on her hair and face. Hair in curlers, finished off with a head scarf. Then came pan-cake, rouge, lipstick, eye-brow pencil and shadow, the lot. Then she got into bed.

'This led to considerable speculation and discussion among the rest of us until we could stand it no longer; we must find out what motivated her. It was decided that I should be the one to enquire whilst the remainder of the watch stood around, ears straining to catch her reply. I waited until she had finished then put the question: "Why do you go to all this trouble before going to bed?" Her reply, "Well, y'never know, y'know," was not exactly enlightening; it left us more perplexed than ever.'

Firewoman Marion Draper was stationed at Blackpool. 'All female staff,' said Marion, 'were billeted in nearby boarding houses and our dining room was in the basement. Food was rationed, of course, and we seemed to be permanently hungry. The cooks did their best with what was available but one cook was a chain smoker, always with a fag dangling from her lips. After seeing the ash from her cigarette fall into the pot of stew she was cooking, we all went out to eat whenever she was on duty.'

But, by and large, the cooks did a good job in difficult circumstances. Food was strictly rationed and, often, had to be prepared over paraffin burners when gas and electricity had been cut off by bombing.

Later in the war, a lady VIP visited a small fire station where she was invited to stay for lunch. After an enjoyable meal, she asked to inspect the kitchen and was taken to a small, hot room. Congratulating the firewoman cook, she asked, 'However did you manage to make such a delicious pastry in this hot little kitchen?' 'No trouble at all, madam,' came the reply. 'When we have important visitors like yourself, I just pop over to the mortuary and use one of the marble slabs; nice and cool in there.'

Gradually, auxiliary stations settled into a routine moulded by their circumstances. Drivers and DRs got to know the ground and their way to neighbouring stations with high fire risk premises. Firewomen became familiar with telephone switchboards and the method of recording fire situations. The communications and mobility exercises had served their purpose and so the drive to prepare staff for action eased a little.

Time hung heavily in some quarters and practical joking was rife. The girls were a natural target for the men, who seemed to have it all their own way in the early days. But the girls hit back unexpectedly and there were a few reversals as the girls found ways of turning the tables. Firewoman Peggy White who was attached to London Fire Brigade HQ Control, was initiated into the intricacies of pump drill in the yard at Lambeth. 'Some of our instructors took a fiendish delight in suddenly increasing the pressure at hose drill, shooting us up in the air at the end of a branch, but we got our own back and gave them all a drink—accidentally, of course. But as time passed and with the coming of the common danger, all prejudice was forgotten and a wonderful camaraderie took its place.'

Firewoman Gilly Giles enlisted at Surbiton; then came a transfer to Imber Court. 'The firemen were always up to tricks,' said Gilly. 'One night, just before black out time, they stuffed some sacks down the chimney of our quarters, hoping to smoke us out. But we had lit a good fire and the sacks caught light and so did our chimney. I and another firewomen took a stirrup pump and a bucket of water up to the roof but our station officer came and ordered us down and sent up a man.'

Whilst at Surbiton, Gilly had organised a dance and raffle, only to find herself transferred to Thames Ditton the day before the event was to take place. Was she dismayed? Not a bit. Obviously, a young lady of considerable initiative, some might say downright cheek, she 'arranged' for a pump to stand by at Surbiton and for herself to be a member of the crew! So she was there for the dance.

After all that, there is no award for guessing who won first prize in the raffle. 'No,' said Gilly, 'it was NOT a fiddle.'

Firewoman Peggy White again. 'The watch room attendants were particularly hostile. They thought we would eventually take over their jobs at a lower rate. Our instructors at squad drill were ex-merchant navy men and their language was distinctly "naval" at time. "Get yer webs orf the deck," was shouted at us as we valiantly tried to mark time in unison and I don't know how many times were "all mogadored".'

Firewoman Marie Thompson's drill instructor was an ex-Army Sergeant, at times disposed to revert to the use of basic English. Said Marie: 'After an exercise which did not please him he called us "a lot of bloody wilting daffodils." But we responded to his instruction and realised how necessary it was when we came up against the

ATS, the WRNS and the WAAF etc. No room for wilting daffodils in that class!'

As time passed and the enemy failed to appear, some members of the public became critical of the Civil Defence Services. One AFS woman DR, held up at traffic lights, heard a man remark to his companion, 'Waste of bloody petrol.' The AFS men were christened 'The darts brigade' and a small boy told a fireman at the fire station gate, 'My Dad says you are a waste of money.'

'The first months of the "phoney" war were a lullaby to what came after and our previous popularity with the public began to wane,' continued Peggy White. '"Two pounds a week for doing nothing" was sometimes shouted after us in the streets. But we were not idle; far from it!'

Some AFS men became fed up with these remarks and resigned from the fire service to join the Armed Forces. Some women may well have done likewise.

In the spring of 1940, morale was sagging and various schemes were created to overcome the trend. Squad drill for women had been included in the curriculum and proved so popular that competitions between squads were arranged. This entailed special training and competition among the girls for places in the teams became intense. Pump drill, too, was very popular among the younger women. It was never envisaged that women would be employed in firefighting with major appliances but it was foreseen that with all fire appliances away from the station attending air raid fires, a knowledge of pump drill among the women might be the means of saving the building. And the girls took it up with a will, setting some most creditable times for a set drill.

Physical training also proved popular and attracted many girls to an activity they had never considered before joining the service. And, of course, the team work involved in all these pursuits cemented the camaraderie already so apparent.

Dances were arranged for the evenings and theatrical groups and repertory companies were organised. These became very popular, not only among the players, but also among audiences.

No. 36 Area had two concert parties, 'Twenty-three on Parade', (after No. 23 station, Homerton) and the semi-professional 'Blitz and Pieces' Company which travelled extensively entertaining audiences from the Armed Forces in addition to Fire Service personnel. There was a tremendous amount of talent available in the AFS; comedians, vocalists, comedy sketches, illusionists, dancers etc., and a number of members of the Companies turned professional after the war. Both shows provided excellent entertainment and their concerts were always packed out.

Audience participation was always cultivated in professional shows. Who can forget the Christmas Pantomime Dame shouting at the audience, 'Oh no he didn't' and the kids all yelling back, 'Oh yes he did'? Fire service audiences never needed prompting in this respect. During the lighter entertainment, repartee was freely exchanged between cast and audience, often with hilarious results. One example transformed the performance of an underwater ballet scene in the show 'On Parade'.

A screen of green gauze was stretched across the stage opening and the area behind it dimly lit to simulate the background for an underwater ballet scene. The senior woman officer was partnered by a regular officer in what had become a very well rehearsed and popular act. Then the male officer was promoted to a rank in which he felt it *infra dig* to continue with the act. With a show coming up the woman officer, very annoyed at the loss of her partner, persuaded her husband to step in at short notice.

Quite apart from the lack of rehearsal, hubby was a 'C' class man, fit only for watch room duties. He also was a trifle breathless and running slightly to fat, a condition very inadequately concealed by his swimsuit.

Firewomen Connie Hunt and Kitty Rushdon appearing in 'Blitz and Pieces'.

The first tableau passed without fault but hubby lacked the flexibility of his predecessor and loud slaps of flesh striking solid flesh began to be heard as she leapt into his arms. One collision was more than poor hubby could withstand and he ended up lying on his back, she sitting on his face.

This was the cue for audience intervention. 'Don't you know it's rude to speak with your mouth full,' was the first crack. His struggle to get her off his face led to a fit of coughing and a further comment, 'Poor old bloke, he's got a touch of asthma,' followed by another: 'No 'e ain't, 'e's swallowed a mouthful o' seaweed.'

The curtain fell mercifully on the scene to avoid further embarrassment and, sadly, to work the final performance of what had been an entertaining little act.

CHAPTER THREE

The Enemy in our Skies

O N 10 May 1940, Hitler began his offensive; the 'phoney' war was over. His troops swept across Europe and one by one Britain's Allies fell before the might of German arms. The British Forces were driven back towards Dunkirk where, between 27 May and 3 June, over 300,000 British and French troops were evacuated from the beaches and brought back to England, largely through the efforts of the armada of 'little ships', one of which was the London Fireboat, *Massey Shaw*.

These were days of foreboding in the control rooms and, indeed, throughout the country. The news from France grew darker as the days passed and the unspoken thoughts of many dwelt on the possibility of facing up to the fury of the *Luftwaffe*. However, firewomen had worked hard and long and were as ready as they could be made for the coming of the bombers.

With the capitulation of France the *Luftwaffe* intensified its attacks on Britain. Throughout June and July, shipping in the Channel and in the Thames estuary was their main target. Then, the attack was switched to the RAF fighter aerodromes on the outskirts of London.

Croydon Aerodrome was attacked on 15 August, the day when the *Luftwaffe* lost seventy-five aircraft in combat and a further fifteen as they returned damaged to their home stations. The ensuing days saw sharp attacks by a hundred-plus bomber formations on fighter aerodromes in the south. The towns of Portsmouth and Ramsgate were among those suffering severe damage and casualties. A devastating attack on the Vauxhall motor works at Luton on the 27th resulted in forty fatal casualties and many injured.

Firewoman Gladys Gunner had been on continuous duty since Dunkirk. Said Gladys, 'We worked three shifts and were required to report to Edmonton Fire Station on the sirens or, at night, on receipt of the "purple". We were picked up by staff car from our homes, many of us barely able to keep our eyes open—slacks over pyjamas—no make up—curlers dragged out—bleary eyed and yawning. Often, on arrival at the station we were told, "Air raid message White; you may return home." But one night, during the early hours, I was standing by the door waiting to be dismissed when, without warning, there was a tremendous explosion, followed by two more in quick succession and the entire station shook. I had never heard a bomb explode before and I heard someone shout, "This is it".

'I heard the appliances start up and everyone dived for their positions. The overall picture was like a disturbed ants nest. The once bleary eyed, yawning group were now wide awake and on the ball. A phone rang and I took the call, reporting a fall of high explosive bombs in Fore Street, Edmonton. I lived in Fore Street and how I took that message I shall never know. How I kept fear out of my voice as I repeated the message I shall also never know. In that moment, I think we all grew up. Thankfully, my home was undamaged but our local cinema and other buildings were wrecked. Although we had no further bombing until 7 September, there was plenty of activity and every "purple" was treated with respect. Every night, the control room buzzed with life; pumps were moved up and closed in. The station was full of personnel, both on and off duty, all on the top line, with pencils poised. We were all part of a team.'

The Admiralty Oil Depot at Pembroke Dock was the target for a heavy attack on 19 August. Fires were started which burned for

seventeen days and cost the lives of five firefighters. Firewoman
Hack Harding said, 'Many men from Cardiff were sent to Pembroke
Dock, including my husband. They had a terrible time, being
machine gunned by enemy planes. When they returned to the station
they came by ambulance and fire service transport. The walking
cases looked very rough, others even worse. My husband, like many,
suffered from fuel oil poisoning which also affected their skin; no
shaving for weeks.'

The raid on the City of London on 25 August, when a number of
fires were started in the Cheapside—Wood Street area, near St Paul's
Cathedral, resulted from a navigational error by German air crews, a
mistake that had a profound effect on the outcome of the war.

This was the first attack on London and Mr Churchill ordered a
reprisal raid on Berlin. It was a feeble effort so far as casualties and
damage was concerned but the effect on German morale was stun-
ning. When the war began, Goering had assured the German people
that an air raid on Berlin could never happen, and they believed
him. Their disillusionment, therefore, was all the greater when British
bombs fell on the German capital. None was more affronted than
the Fuehrer himself. In a speech in Berlin he vowed vengeance
'night for night. If they attack our cities we will erase theirs.'

So, against the advice of Hermann Goering and some of his senior
commanders, the *Luftwaffe*'s attack on RAF fighter aerodromes,
which was inflicting such enormous damage on our defence capacity,
was abandoned in favour of an all out attack on London.

The recent skirmishes had given the fire services a taste of things
to come, although it was to be a few days before the full significance
of the Prime Minister's promise of 'Blood and tears; toil and sweat'
materialised.

The great oil refineries at Shellhaven and Thameshaven at the
mouth of the River Thames were bombed and set on fire on
5 September, thus providing many of the Auxiliary Firemen, and

regulars, too, with their first sight of a major oil fire. In the control rooms, firewomen were not marking their message forms 'Exercise'; this was the real thing.

Firewoman 'Nobby' Clarke was instructed to join a requisitioned vehicle, a removal van complete with civilian driver, bound for Thameshaven. 'We girls,' said Nobby, 'were disgusted that we had no vehicle to drive but we had been instructed that we belonged to a disciplined service and so turned to without demur. The van was not equipped for service as a canteen van, just carried a few thermos urns, two primus stoves, a supply of fresh water and stores. On arrival at Thameshaven we were given a parking place and set up business. Our driver thereupon vanished, to reappear when the "all clear" sounded next morning. The HQ staff had filled our urns with tea which we served with biscuits until supplies ran out, after which we made cocoa.

'During the night we were continually bombed and machine gunned and it became clear why we had been issued with tin hats. We found the hissing of the primus stoves comforting; the noise drowned the scream of the bombs and the rattle of machine guns. Whilst the activity continued we were all alert and wide awake. We served biscuits and mugs of tea to weary firemen, their saturated uniforms smelling to high heaven with smoke, oil and foam; the excitement of a bomber screaming down in a dive with machine guns firing, and the glare and smell of the blazing oil tanks. But as the first gleam of daylight appeared we realised that the bombers had gone and we all suddenly felt completely washed out.'

Sirens sounded across the capital on the following night, when a small force of bombers attacked targets on the outskirts, including the Royal Docks and Silvertown, causing some damage and casualties. The activity kept control room personnel busy until 0400 hrs on the Saturday morning.

CHAPTER FOUR

'Fires were Started'

THE watch at Abbey Road turned to at 0700 hrs, all a bit bleary-eyed from lack of sleep. There was considerable business to complete during the morning, and, after lunch, as many as could be spared crept away to catch up on sleep. Then, at about 5.00 p.m. came the Air Raid message 'Purple', swiftly followed by the 'Red' and the sounding of the sirens.

Suddenly, it seemed, the air was filled with the noise of hundreds of bombers, a fearsome, menacing roar. Then came the bark of anti-aircraft gunfire and the deeper thud of exploding bombs. A stricken bomber came circling down to crash on a garden shelter in Ranelagh Road, West Ham, killing all the occupants but an infant who was rescued by women living nearby. The Ford Motor Works at Dagenham, the Beckton Gas works and large area of the Royal Docks, including several ships, had been set alight by the German incendiaries. Bombers flew along the great line of factories stretching from North Woolwich to Tidal Basin; soap works, sugar refineries, timber yards, paint factories, tar distilleries and chemical factories, scattering high explosive and incendiary bombs. Molten pitch from the tar distillery flooded the North Woolwich Road, halting all traffic. A squadron of bombers detached from the main force swept over the Surrey Commercial Docks, the country's major soft-timber importing centre. Within minutes large areas of the 250 acres of timber stacks were blazing. On swept the bombers, aiming their high explosives and incendiaries at warehouses and factories lining the river banks from North Woolwich to Tower Bridge.

In the fire control rooms, the period of make believe had come to a sudden end and all were brought face to face with the violent reality of bombardment from the air. No longer were control room personnel dealing with simulated incidents involving ten or twenty pumps; the messages they were now receiving reported dreadful tragedies and enormous damage. The worst hit areas were calling for assistance measured in hundreds of pumps. Bombs were falling in close proximity to many East End fire controls, shaking buildings and bringing down plaster from ceilings. Many stations were without electricity or telephone communication. Candles were the usual form of secondary lighting and despatch riders set out to establish communication links between vital points.

The intense training had paid off. Firewomen at the switchboards and telephones followed routine procedure but found it necessary to bring all their concentration to bear on the task in hand in face of all the noise and confusion and danger; in so doing, they managed to ward off distracting thoughts from their minds.

After the initial shock, personnel settled down to more or less normal routine. Fire stations had been emptied of their appliances in the first few minutes of the attack although calls for assistance continued to flood in from street fire alarms, telephones and the air raid wardens. All calls were recorded and passed to the District Control for attention.

Firewoman Lilian Borne had been off duty when the sirens sounded. She saw her mother to the shelter and then made her way back to Stratford fire station. On her way she saw the Kinema in West Ham Lane in ruins following a direct hit and a great gap in Queen Mary's Hospital, with a gas main blazing nearby. A pump from Stratford passed on its way to the West Ham Corporation yard, where three firemen and six ARP workers had been killed by one of the first bombs to fall. Said Lilian, 'It was more like Charing Cross railway station than Stratford fire station. Fire crews were reporting in from all directions in response to our calls for help. I began to collect all the message slips and transfer them to the blackboard and eventually got the Occurrence Book up to date. During the evening, a young RAF man was carried into the watch room with blood spurting from a wound in his leg; he had been slashed by glass from a large shop window following a near miss from a high explosive bomb that rocked our station. Firemen rendered first aid and we got him away to hospital. About a fortnight later he came back to thank us for saving his life.'

In the London 'J' Region Control at Abbey Road, West Ham, the district had despatched all available pumps in the first few minutes. One of the first bombs had cut the electricity supply and mobilising was continued by the light of candles stuck in jam jars. Dagenham, Barking and East Ham were all calling for assistance and requests from West Ham for reinforcing pumps moved towards the five hundred mark, as reports of the conflagration in the Royal Docks filtered in. Many telephone lines were cut and we relied on despatch riders, many of them women, to maintain links with officers on the fireground. Requests for assistance were passed to Regional Fire Control at Lambeth who ordered reinforcements from unaffected areas of the Region.

The Regional Fire Officer, Commander A.N.G. Firebrace CBE, who was in the control room, thought that the West Ham officers had the bit between their teeth and were requesting an excessive number of pumps. Accordingly, he despatched two of his staff officers to survey the area. After a hair raising journey around the hot spots, spending nearly four hours exposed to some of the worst bombing and narrowly escaping being cut off by fire, they arrived back at 'J' Control and told the mobilising officer that they thought 1,000 pumps could be justified.

Gladys Gunner had been given the day off to attend the wedding of a special friend. 'I was at the reception at Tottenham when the

Red alert at the London Fire Brigade HQ Control. Commander Firebrace and his staff sit before the fire situation board. On occasions, staff members were sent to assess an obscure situation.

The clusters of pegs on the board represent pumps available in each London district and local fire brigade area. The fw. on the right adjust the peg board as the fire situation develops. Company Officer Margaret Davis, senior woman fire officer, stands ready to adjust the pegs showing the fire situation in any area. The telephone cubicles are extended along the left of the control room. Every single pump of the Region's vast resources was actively engaged in firefighting and reinforcement had to be requested from the Home Office fire control.

warning sounded and we all trooped outside and watched the sky over the Thames become filled with what looked like flies and it dawned on us that they were bombers, knocking hell out of the docks. I felt like a fish out of water and I knew I had to get back to my station. No sign of a bus, of course, so I set out on a four mile walk. Planes were buzzing overhead and the streets were deserted. Guns were firing and I could hear bombs dropping in the distance and there was something strangely unreal about the situation. As daylight faded, the sky seemed to glow more intensely red so that I never noticed the blackout. As I reached the station I saw that it was completely empty; not a single appliance at home. I made my way to the control room where, instead of the usual buzz of conversation there was silence. The girls were recovering from a hectic period of activity, ordering appliances from all over the district to the great conflagrations in the docks, and adjusting to the trauma of recent events.

'The mobilising officer said to me, "Just pray we get no further calls for there is not a single pump in the district." I have never felt so helpless or frustrated in all my life. We just sat and looked at one another.'

South of the River Thames, the great area of timber stacks in the Surrey Commercial Docks at Rotherhithe had received special attention from the *Luftwaffe*. Watchers in the yard at Pageant's Wharf fire station adjoining the dock saw a squadron of bombers detach itself from the main body and make for the timber. Thousands of incendiary bombs came raining down on the closely built stacks whilst high explosives ripped many of them apart. Fire spread with incredible speed, aided by oil and magnesium fire bombs and the accumulation of wood chips built up over decades.

The bombs were seen to drop by Station Officer Knight and his men standing in the yard at Pageant's Wharf fire station. They turned out immediately and were at the scene within a few minutes of the explosions.

Three firewomen were on duty in the control room that afternoon. They notified their District Control at New Cross that their appliances were out to Surrey Commercial Docks and then calls started to pour in. Each was recorded and passed to New Cross with the message, 'No attendance from this station'. Said Firewoman

Bessie Barrett, 'The bombing seemed incessant, the screaming of the high explosives and the whoosh of the incendiaries. The three of us were so busy answering the phones, taking in calls and keeping our district station informed, that we had no time to be scared. We were unable to leave the watch room, not even to visit the loo; we "went" in a bucket behind the fire alarm cabinet.

'After about an hour there was a pause in the bombing and the "all clear" sounded. But it did not last long. They were soon back in force and the bombs again rained down. We began to wonder how long it would be before we stopped one. Our greatest worry was the oil depot adjoining the station and we really had the wind up wondering what might happen if it was hit. One of us just had to pop out to see if it had escaped when there was a close one that shook the station.

'Darkness had fallen but the sky was a bright pink colour, with clouds of golden sparks drifting over the station and across the river. The whole station had filled with the blue haze of burning wood, bringing tears to our eyes and irritating our noses and throats. The bombing continued all night until dawn came at about 5.30 a.m. when, thankfully, we heard the sirens sound the all clear.'

AGO Doris Tyler was on duty at Bethnal Green fire station when the sirens sounded. 'My memories of that night are vague. It was the end of one period in our lives; the next incredible phase had begun. Looking back, it was quite amazing how quickly we became accustomed to blitz conditions. We felt a bit edgy when the "Yellow" message came in but as soon as the "Red" was received and the sirens sounded, it was almost as if we had been "programmed" to deal with situations as they developed. I was conscious of explosions, some near, others more distant, but they were merely a background to the bewildering thoughts that filled my mind. Our training had prepared us for the flood of calls and now we were face to face with reality. Our appliances were sent to answer the first call, after that all calls were recorded and sent to our District Control at Whitechapel. My concentration was such that the noise of the bombing was subdued but I am quite unable to remember details.'

Firewoman Bridget Harris was attached to Knightsbridge Fire Station in London's West End. When her station officer was ordered to take charge of a fire at the Victoria Naval Dockyard in Deptford, Bridget was standing ready with the staff car. As they neared Deptford, the glare from the burning timber stacks in the Surrey Docks lit streets as brightly as day. The Dockyard buildings were well alight as Bridget pulled up. 'As I got out of the car,' she said, 'a series of explosions caused me to duck down behind the car. After a while, I realised they were coming from the interior of the burning building and were not, as I had at first thought, a new German weapon. Later, I heard that cans of surgical spirit were exploding from the heat in the medical store. Fortunately for us, the rum store remained intact.'

'The blitz became a mass of incidents; fact and fiction seemed to merge,' said Firewoman Gladys Gunner. 'The feeling of utter help-lessness when all the appliances were out at the dock fires and we had nothing more to offer. The biggest struggle was with oneself; to appear nonchalant at all times despite the inward belief that one came from a long line of cowards. To receive a report during the raid that a parachutist had been sighted coming our way and to pass on the message without hitting top "C" was a feat of self control. The "parachutist" turned out to be a land mine, caught by its parachute cords in a tree opposite our station; yet another scare to add to our mounting store of them.'

'On the opening night of the blitz I was on leave,' said Firewoman Peggy White. 'I had been to the wedding of a colleague and formed part of the guard of honour. When the sirens sounded I made for home but our tram was stopped at New Cross Depot and all passengers were ordered into a public shelter. But being in uniform,

I was allowed to continue and belted for home. We spent the night in the Anderson Shelter listening to the drone of bombers and the barrage of gunfire. I had to be on duty at 7.00 a.m. next morning. I remember the streets being comparatively quiet. Our district had not seen the worst of the bombing and there was very little private motoring then. Everybody turned up, if not exactly on time, despite the fact that girls had to travel from all parts of London.

'The control was a hive of activity and remained so all day. There was no time to swap "bomb stories" or even to gain information, apart from handing over duties. Some senior officers, in full fire fighting gear, smelling of smoke and looking tired and grimy, were studying the mobilising boards. They always went on to major fires. The Occurrence Book work was overwhelming, as hundreds of messages were received at HQ that night. On some of the subsequent heavier raids, the Occurrence Book never was brought up to date.

'Both Blue and Red Watches had been on duty all night. No firewoman had fainted, panicked or gone hysterical, as had been predicted by some. The Regional Fire Officer had complimented Group Officer Margaret Davies on the exemplary behaviour of the firewomen under her control on their "baptism of fire". The fact was that we had become so disciplined by our perpetual and much grumbled at daily exercises that when the real thing came it went "just like an exercise".'

Wheathampstead, a small village a few miles north of St Albans, is the home of Helmets Ltd, a works specialising in the manufacture of helmets for troops fighting in the tropics. The firm also made peacetime helmets for the larger brigades so it was natural that the work force volunteered, in a part-time capacity, for the AFS. Said Firewoman Muriel Arnold, 'We were accommodated in a small room adjoining the fire station. We were drilled and trained in firefighting and felt so confident that we entered for pump competitions in various parts of the County. We were very enthusiastic,

This is the happy group of part-timers
from Helmets Limited, Wheathampstead.

proudly wearing our uniforms although we knew it was unlikely that we should have to attend a large fire. On the first night of the blitz, we stood on the hill at the back of our station watching the glow of the dock fires burning twenty-five miles away. We had the odd salvo of fire bombs, jettisoned by a fleeing aircraft and a couple of stray doodle-bugs, but few other incidents to report. But we stood ready to do our duty if called upon and felt we were doing out little bit for the war effort.'

'Although I was on watch room duties most of the time,' said Firewoman Majorie Watkins, 'I was also a registered driver and occasionally drove a staff car. One afternoon, after a night of heavy bombing, a fireman reported to Stratford Fire Station with two pumps from Clacton. He was instructed to report to the Royal Victoria Dock but had no idea how to get there. There was no DR available so I took the staff car and acted as guide. After a nightmare journey trying to find undamaged roads, with bomb rubble everywhere, I eventually arrived in Silvertown and left my charges there. On the way back to Stratford, I was flagged down by a PC. "You can't go down there," he said, "there's an unexploded bomb." It was one of the roads I had negotiated only ten minutes earlier.'

Firewoman Mitzi Spooner was stationed at 37 Z sub-station, an ancient school in Dalston, East London. 'We had had a heavy fall of incendiaries in the area and were quite busy,' said Mitzi. 'It was getting dark so I went to light the gas. As I am only five feet tall, I had to stand on a chair and had just grasped the chain which turned on the gas tap when we had a near miss and I came flying off the chair, still holding the chain. The result was I fell heavily and felt a sharp pain in my ankle, but that did not worry me so much as the fact that I had broken the gas mantle, an item in very short supply and difficult to replace. I finished up in the Metropolitan Hospital with a fractured ankle but, compared to injuries other people were being brought in with, I couldn't complain.'

The east London river-side boroughs were receiving heavy punishment from the bombers. Thousands of people were made homeless; a few made their own arrangements for re-housing but the majority relied upon the Local Authority to make the necessary arrangements. There were pitiful scenes at rest centres as bombed out people were brought in. Not only had their homes been destroyed; many of them had suffered family bereavement and were inconsolable. Through all their distress, anguish and shock, some had managed to rescue the family pet, a dog or cat, and clung pathetically to the animal as they huddled together, awaiting news of their transfer to a safer area.

Firewoman Bessie Butler at Pageant's Wharf fire station received news at 2.30 a.m. that her home had been bombed. Quite apart from their ordeal on the first night of the blitz, she and her colleagues on the Blue Watch were distressed by the news of the death of their popular Station Officer 'Gerrie' Knight, killed on the second night of the attack on the Surrey Docks.

Said Bessie, 'We had been sent a replacement station officer and he sent me home by staff car. I found the house in ruins but my parents were reported safe. They had been sent to a rest centre but the Civil Defence people were unable to tell me where. There was nothing I could do at that time of night so I returned to the fire station, now my temporary home. Next morning I was given leave to find my parents and help with arrangements for their rehousing. I found they had been sent to a rest centre at Dartford and there were a few tears as we were reunited. I sent telegrams to my brothers in the Forces so as to get them home on leave to help and then I tried to salvage what I could from our home. Then off to the Borough Housing Department, to arrange for my parents to be rehoused. By this time it was getting dark and I decided to make my way back to the station before the sirens sounded. But they were early this evening and I was about half a mile from the station when I heard a big one coming down. I lay flat in the roadway and covered my head with my hands as a tremendous explosion occurred. I was struck all over my body with shrapnel but it did not hurt as much as I expected. After a moment, I opened my eyes and looked around. The road was littered with potatoes, onions, carrots and all sorts of vegetables and this was the shrapnel that had pummelled me. The greengrocers, just along the road from where I was lying, had received a direct hit. I dusted myself down and started to run for the station before I became the target for something a bit more deadly.'

Across the river in West Ham, firemen were returning to the stations with household pets; dogs, cats, budgies, etc., rescued from

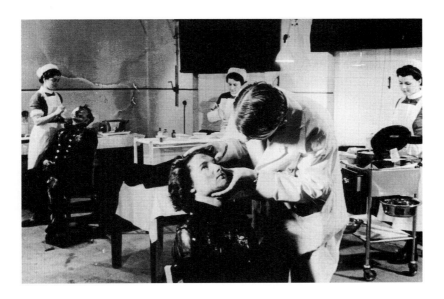

In the casualty ward at Westminster Hospital. Fire service peronnel receive treatment for eye injuries caused by showers of sparks driven by the fierce fire winds. Very painful.

bombed buildings. Some of the occupiers had been killed, others detained in hospital so the firemen brought the pets back to the station as a temporary home. 'The soft-hearted firewomen took over,' said Firewoman Marjorie Watkins, 'caring for them until they were returned to their owners or a new home could be found. One night, a white bull terrier was brought in. He wasn't very white when he arrived, having been dug out of the rubble, but a bath with plenty of soft soap restored him to his natural colour. As he became used to living in the fire station, we sat him on a stool in the watch room, put a duty belt around him and called him Fireman Bill. He loved all the attention he was given and took to chasing after the fire appliances when they turned out. He often rode home in state on the machine and became a great favourite with everyone. Old Bill was a happy memory and found fame when his name was entered in the Occurrence Book: Fireman Bill on duty. We hoped nobody too high up got round to checking the book but by this time, the firewomen had proved their worth and were left to get on with the job. Eventually, Bill found a loving home with one of the cooks.'

'What a change in the attitude of the public to the fire service after a few weeks of the blitz,' said Firewoman Peggy White. 'It was now pats on the back and an occasional apple or rare orange from the golden hearted cockneys of Lambeth Walk. No more talk of money for doing nothing.'

AGO Doris Tyler remembers checking in pumps reporting from Cambridge, Southend, etc. 'We had so many calls from Mile End Road that it seemed the whole road must be alight. So we directed the pumps on there and instructed the crews to get stuck into the first fire they came across.

'On 10 September we sent out our crews, as usual, a few minutes after the first bombs fell. One of the pumps had not returned next morning but this was not unusual. It had not returned by late afternoon and we began to worry. Then we received a message that our pump had been reported missing; we lived in hope but feared the worst. Next morning, the wife of one of the boys came to ask why he had not come home on what was his leave day. What could we tell her?

'It was a few days before we learned that the pump and its entire crew had been wiped out. By that time we were prepared for the news but it still came as a shock. I cannot remember a single woman showing any fear, but there were a few tears when the news of our pump was confirmed.'

On the night of 20 September 1940, Firewoman Gillian (Bobby) Tanner was instructed to load her van with 150 gallons of petrol in two gallon cans. She set off from Dockhead fire station, across London Bridge and through streets lined with blazing buildings, with all the noise and menace of an air raid in full blast. Shrapnel from anti-aircraft guns rattled on the pavements but, undeterred, Bobbie drove on through the dock gates towards the inferno that was her destination.

It was an awe inspiring sight. Great warehouses along the dockside blazed as small groups of firemen wrestled with powerful jets of water that seemed to make no impression on the flames. Clouds of golden sparks rose high into the sky, carried aloft by the terrific heat upcast as enemy aircraft cruised menacingly overhead. She reported to a control officer and was instructed to deliver her fuel to a section of pumps working on the quayside.

Each can weighed about 17 lbs and Bobbie carried her petrol from pump to pump topping up the tanks, a dangerous task calling for great care since the glowing hot exhaust manifold lay only inches from the tank filler-cap. Such an operation calls for a steady hand and nerve at the best of times, much more so with the distraction of being under attack by enemy bombers. One careless move or a blast from a nearby explosion would have splashed petrol over the manifold with disastrous results. After a period of considerable physical exertion and nerve-wracking effort, all the fuel was distributed, whereupon she collected up the empty cans and returned them to her station.

It was an outstanding act of bravery on the part of a twenty-one year old girl. Bobbie herself, after it was all over, remarked, 'However did I get away with it?'

The *London Gazette* (31 January 1941) carried the following citation:

Gillian Tanner, Auxiliary Fire Service, Awarded the George Medal.
Six serious fires were in progress and for three hours Auxiliary Firewoman Tanner drove a 30 cwt. lorry loaded with 150 gallons of petrol from fire to fire, replenishing petrol supplies to the fire

Firewoman Bobbie Tanner, seen with her mother outside Buckingham Palace
after being invested with the George Medal by H.M. King George VI.

pumps despite intense bombing at the time. She showed remarkable
coolness and courage throughout.

Firewoman Gladys Birchmore: 'We took each night of bombing
as it occurred and it was good to be busy. I found it worse on leave
days when I tried to catch up on sleep. We lived near Wormwood
Scrubs and at night Big Bertha would do her best to get Jerry before
he got us. During the blitz and the dock fires, duty was continuous
and my twenty-first birthday was swallowed up in one hectic thirty-
six hour stretch.'

Firewoman Win Hunt was a Dispatch Rider attached to 20Y
West Hampstead fire station. 'It had been a very busy night in the
Edgware Road area and I was kept on the run with dispatches from
our pumps to the station. I had just passed Edgware Road fire station
when my front wheel went down a hole in the road and I went

October 7th, 1940. Soho fire station after a direct hit. Standing instructions were that all off-duty personnel were to take shelter in the basement on an alert, but Station Officer Bill Wilson and Auxiliary fireman Fred Mitchell were catching up on paper work in an upper office when the bomb struck. Those sheltering in the basement were quickly released, but staff in the Control Room (behind the arched window on the right of the photograph) found their exit blocked by debris which took some time to clear before they could be released. It was two days before the bodies of Wilson and Mitchell were recovered.

over the top of the bike and landed on my face. I managed to pick myself up and straighten out the handlebars before pushing the bike to the fire station. The girls were very good, attending to my face which was very painful, and brought me tea. They took my dispatch and telephoned it to my station, telling them they were keeping me at Edgware Road until daybreak. I was determined to ride the bike back to 20Y which I managed to do. My face was now badly swollen and I was placed on the sick list, but returned to duty after three days.'

'Our station, No. 82 Old Kent Road, was right in the thick of things; we were never hit, although we had a number of near misses,' said Firewoman Vera Burnand. 'Some of the nights were very frightening and on the busier nights I remember the firemen coming home after hours of firefighting, soaking wet and absolutely exhausted. They sat on the floor, leaning against the appliance room walls and simply fell asleep until the next call came in and out they went again.'

Win Mercer joined up at Tooting and although a driver, was sent for training as a dispatch rider. 'They put me on a Singer 250cc,' said Win, 'and, later, changed it to a big 500cc Panther bike from the USA. These were too heavy for women; one of our girls was killed on one so they took us off them. After several different jobs in the AFS I was put on canteen van work. I don't drink tea and I am afraid the tea I served the firemen was not up to expectation; in fact they were always complaining about "my rotten tea."

'The problem was that we were issued with only ½lb tea, 2 tins of Carnation milk and 2lbs of sugar to make a hundred mugs of tea. I was really upset at the complaints I received and told my mother about it. She gave me a small packet of bicarbonate of soda and told me how to use it.

'What a transformation! From thereon, I served the strongest tea and had the healthiest firemen in the brigade. Whenever I turned

A canteen van, presented to the NFS by the Canadian Red Cross, with its crew on parade in LFB Headquarters yard, Lambeth, 18 March 1942. Assistant Fire Force Commander Ronnie Greene and Fire Force Commander Geoffrey Blackstone in attendance.

up in the blitz area with my van, they rushed over for a "cup of Win's nectar!"'

Firewoman A. Baxter was posted to Soho and enjoyed the bustle and activity of a busy fire station. 'I didn't mind the long hours,' she said, 'there was always something to do, as Soho was one of the busiest stations, even before the air raids started. I was more nervous when I was on leave, sitting in the shelter listening to the bombs coming down. We were kept fully occupied during a raid, even when our appliances were out. We used the stirrup pumps to put out incendiary bomb fires burning near our station. Several of our men were badly burned and detained in Charing Cross Hospital, where we used to visit them on our leave days and help the nurses out by feeding the lads who were so heavily bandaged that they could not feed themselves.'

Firewoman Joan Jones remembers the busy nights at the beginning of the blitz. 'We had the Municipal Ambulances at the Croydon main station and you could bet your life that as soon as an air raid got under way we would receive a call for an ambulance for a maternity case. We always felt sorry for the poor girl on her way to the maternity hospital with guns firing, bombs dropping and all the rest of the din.'

Firewoman Nobby Clarke had been transferred from Hammersmith to Headquarters. 'I was detailed to standby to take out a canteen van. This turned out to be a London bus, complete with driver and conductor, a condition imposed by the bus company. We had thermos urns of hot cocoa and great stacks of mugs. Three firewomen made up the crew and we made the conductor the pot-man; his job was to collect the empties. We were ordered out to Deptford and as we got close to our destination more and more roads were blocked by "Diversion" signs. That usually meant a bomb crater or a UXB, unexploded bomb. I soon learned that London bus drivers, once away from their usual routes, were completely lost. Ours kept asking, "Where now?" when we had to detour and we girls had to act as guides. We got ourselves into a position where the only way forward was to pull aside the diversion sign and proceed. I walked in front and my colleagues walked on either side of the bus. We soon discovered the reason for the diversion, a great land mine lying at the side of the road with its parachute draped all around. The bus stopped and we had a consultation. You can't manoeuvre a bus like an Austin Seven; we couldn't go back so we decided to push on. It was only a few days since I had attended a lecture on Magnetic Mines, when we were told that a metal button on a tunic or even a bunch of keys in a pocket were sufficient to set it off. We decided that it could go off whether we were going backwards or forwards. So, the bus crept forward and we held our breaths as we approached, came abreast and then passed the mine.

This parachute mine has been rendered safe by a Naval Mine Disposal Team.
It is similar to that encountered by 'Nobby' Clarke and her canteen van crew
mates when they tried to take a short cut through Deptford streets, except that
theirs was alive and ready to go!

We breathed again after we were well clear but you never heard
such gear grinding as that driver produced as he passed the mine.'

Firewoman Bobbie Tanner GM had been transferred to the
Transport Depot at Avery Hill, Woolwich. Volunteers were called
for to collect a mechanical road-sweeper from Bath to be delivered
to Deptford for clearing roads of debris; Bobbie put her name forward
and was given the job.

'When I saw it, I wondered what I had let myself in for,' said
Bobbie. 'It was a First World War job, with solid rubber tyres and
had a maximum speed of 5mph!' Outside Bath, she gave a lift to a
RAF officer who stuck it for a mile or two then asked to be put
down. 'I'd sooner ride on the wing-tip of my aeroplane,' was his
parting shot.

'The journey took two and a half days,' said Bobbie. 'I spent the first night in Swindon and the next in Slough; I only hope the effort was worthwhile and that it earned its keep in the Deptford streets.'

Firewoman Constance Palmer joined up at the age of eighteen and was attached to Clapham Fire Station. 'We had all kinds of vehicles to drive; American sedans with left hand drive, trade vans and a hearse with gate-change gears. During the blitz I was driving a van which formerly belonged to a biscuit company, carrying stores to my station. Passing Lambeth Fire HQ the engine caught fire. I pulled up and grabbed the fire extinguisher but it was stuck. So I turned out the HQ men who nearly had a fit when they saw it was an AFS vehicle. After all the fuss, I felt rather pleased with myself for having taken a fire to the fire station.'

We had a number of part-time firewomen who reported for duty after finishing their day at the office. I admired these girls immensely. After a hectic night on the switchboard they set out for their offices at 8.00 a.m. through streets littered with debris and broken glass, with little chance of a bus and the prospect of a long walk before them.

The foregoing stories are typical of the events that London based firewomen experienced for fifty-seven consecutive nights. During the first week of September 1940, the attack was concentrated on docks and the great industrial complexes in the East End. Then the enemy extended his operations to cover the whole of the 750 square miles of the Metropolitan area. None of the boroughs escaped damage, although some were worse hit than others.

During this period the *Luftwaffe* also ranged widely over important targets on the mainland from the south coast to the north of Scotland. These were mainly pre-strike reconnaissance, the shape of things to come, but some of the major industrial cities had sharp attacks, causing considerable material damage and casualties. Aircraft factories at Southampton and Filton, Bristol, came in for repeated attack during those early autumn days and nights.

In a statement on 8 October 1940, Prime Minister Winston Churchill told the House of Commons, 'A month has passed since Herr Hitler turned his rage and malice onto the civil population of our great cities and particularly on London . . . When we entered the war we expected to sustain losses which might amount to 3,000 killed in a single night and 12,000 wounded night after night . . . Since the heavy raiding began on 7 September the figures of killed and seriously wounded have declined steadily week by week from over 6,000 in the first week to just under 5,000 in the second, to about 4,000 in the third week and to under 3,000 in the last of the four weeks. The destruction of property has, however, been very considerable. Most painful has been the destruction of small houses inhabited by working folk. We will rebuild them more to our credit than some of them were before. London, Liverpool, Manchester, Birmingham may have much more to suffer . . .'

And so it proved.

At the beginning of October, enemy tactics against London changed. Mass attacks by 200-plus aircraft were replaced by smaller formations, sometimes employing single aircraft or flights of two or three, sometimes as many as thirty, ranging far and wide over the capital and keeping the Civil Defence Services on the alert. These were interspersed with short, sharp attacks when heavy calibre bombs and parachute mines were brought into use. As nights lengthened, London was often under red alert for up to fourteen hours. The aim was to compel people to endure the discomfort of shelter life and deprive them of sleep. This, it was believed by the Germans, would lead to the breakdown of morale and loss of output in the factories.

Although London continued to be the main target, attacks on the Merseyside towns, Birmingham, Cardiff, Southampton, Plymouth, Bristol etc, continued with increasing severity. The enemy was using parachute mines with mounting frequency but not all of those exploded on impact. Heroic work by the Royal Navy experts from HMS Vernon, Portsmouth, successfully defused many. Unhappily, not all were rendered harmless, for the Germans took to inserting new traps in the firing mechanism and a number of mine disposal crews were obliterated.

Birmingham experienced a short, sharp attack on 24 October 1940 when the area around New Street station was damaged. A more severe attack came next night when the city centre was heavily bombed and considerable damage was done.

Firewoman Doris Smith was driver/radio operator to S. H. Todd Divisional Officer E and B Divisions. Said Doris, 'Our headquarters was in Trafalgar Road, Moseley and we had about ten square miles of the city to cover. One fire I attended was at a large factory in Bradford Street. I pulled up in what I thought was a safe position and sat in the car transmitting radio messages. Ahead of me was a turntable ladder at work on the fire with two firemen at the top. Suddenly, the walls of the factory buckled and the fire swept out, engulfing the ladder and the firemen. Nothing but their helmets were found in the debris.

'I knew incidents of this kind were common in wartime but it was my first experience of death and it left me badly shaken. My car was blistered along one side with the heat and I was called over the coals next morning for parking too close to the fire. It taught me a great lesson and I never made the same mistake again.'

November 14 is a date Coventry folk will never forget. For eight hours, 450 heavy bombers attacked the city, dropping 500 tonnes of high explosives and 30,000 incendiary bombs. It was the heaviest attack yet on a British city and enormous damage was done. The attack was not indiscriminate; it was well planned. Under a full moon, the bomb aimers were able to identify and bomb their individual targets without difficulty, much of the heart of the city was destroyed. There was heavy damage to industrial plants, commercial and residential premises.

Public utility services were disrupted together with road, rail and telephone communications. As might be expected, casualties were heavy; nearly 600 people were killed and over 800 seriously injured.

The city's industrial output had been temporarily halted but, with the restoration of the public utility services, the factories swiftly resumed production.

Firewoman Barbara Crosland BEM joined the AFS in October 1939 and was attached to Central Fire Station in Leeds. 'Our quarters were in the West Riding Police Station, adjoining the fire station,' she told me. 'The control room was located in the cells! I vividly remember the Coventry bombing. I reported for duty at 10.00 p.m. that night, armed with my tin hat over one arm and a basket containing a steak and kidney pudding over the other. This was to be my team's supper. We had a small open fireplace in the main office and a heavy iron saucepan to re-heat the pudding.

'When I reached the control room, it was "all stations go". We were despatching every available pump in our district to Nuneaton for water relaying. Needless to say, our pudding wasn't eaten that night!'

Next on the list was Southampton, which suffered an ordeal by fire and high explosives for a fortnight, during which a total of more than 600 people were killed. Then, an extremely serious and damaging attack by 400-plus bombers on Birmingham, resulting in the death of 450 citizens, with 500 seriously injured. Bombing in the Midlands was widespread, with heavy damage and casualties. Heavy damage and casualties in Leicester followed a raid in which two parachute mines were dropped.

Firewoman Doris Smith: 'At about 2.00 a.m. the DO's car was ordered and I drove him to a block of luxury flats. The previous night I had put my hair up in curlers before going to bed and smeared some awful green cream on my face, supposed to be good for the complexion. When the car was ordered I threw on my uniform, rammed my tin hat on top of the curlers and ran out for the car. We arrived at the job and found the roof well alight. DO Todd ran in and I followed with my message pad. As we entered the hall the lift door opened and several American soldiers who were billeted there ran out. I suddenly saw this green apparition coming towards me; my first inclination was to turn and run but I then realised it was my own reflection in the mirror at the back of the lift. No wonder those soldiers looked scared!

'Later, we went on to a private house where an old lady had been burned to death. I followed the DO and was given a message requesting the attendance of the mortuary van and the coroner's officer. The tragedy affected me and as I left the house I started to shake violently and had to ask a fireman to help me with the radio switches. As I transmitted the message my voice seemed so strange that I wondered how the girl at the other end understood. I really had to take a grip on myself before I was fit to drive.'

November 24 saw the heaviest attack, so far, on Bristol. For five hours, bombers rained incendiaries on the city, supplemented by high explosive bombs of the heaviest calibre. Their use was designed to damage water mains and so impede firefighting. There was prior knowledge of this attack and ARP and fire services were drafted into the city beforehand. Water supplies to the city were seriously affected and drinking water had to be brought in by tanker and water cart by the military.

Plymouth and Liverpool/Birkenhead suffered similar treatment later in the month.

Quite apart from local activity, firewomen were kept busy in other areas, mobilising reinforcing columns of fire pumps to go to the assistance of the beleaguered cities. These were accompanied by mobile kitchens, dispatch riders, canteen vans, field telephone units, hose laying vans and ancillary vehicles, almost entirely driven and crewed by firewomen.

The month of December 1940 saw the continuation of the series of attacks on Southampton, followed by further major raids on the cities that had suffered so badly during November; Liverpool/Birkenhead, Bristol, Portsmouth, Birmingham, London. On the night of 12–13 December, Sheffield was the target for over 300 heavy bombers. Three hundred and fifty tonnes of high explosives and more than 16,000 incendiary bombs were dropped in the nine hours the city was under attack. Three days later came the 'follow up' raid. Although not as heavy as the first, severe damage and casualties resulted. A total of 760 citizens of Sheffield died.

Liverpool/Birkenhead was again heavily bombed successively on the nights of 20–21 and 21–22 resulting in severe damage and many casualties.

On the second night, a convoy of pumps from London was sent to Liverpool. Included among the ancillary vehicles was a hose laying lorry driven by a London firewoman. On arrival, she was directed to one of the hot spots but got lost and called in at a fire station to ask the way. The raid was at the height of its fury; bombs dropping, ack ack guns firing, fire bells ringing and all the din of an air raid in full swing. She received her directions and turned towards the door, whereupon the station officer said, 'Hey, hold on, you can't go out in this!' To which she replied, 'Why not. Is it raining?'

Next on the list came Manchester, whose ordeal commenced on the night of 22–23 December and continued the next night. The attacks were devastating and large areas of the commercial centre were set ablaze. Whole blocks of buildings and entire streets were engulfed in flame and such was the glare that it was visible to German pilots flying over London on their way home.

Two days before Christmas Eve, Firewoman Vera Linfield was on duty at London Fire Brigade Headquarters, Lambeth. London had had a few days respite from the *Luftwaffe* and Vera was looking forward to leave the next day and making arrangements for the

A quintet of DRs line up for the photographer.
The masked headlamps projected a dim glow only a few yards ahead; not a great
help on a 200-mile run from London to Manchester in the black-out!

family Christmas. At about 4.00 p.m. she was approached by an
AGO who informed her that Manchester was the target for that
night and Vera was to stock up her canteen van ready to leave with
the convoy of pumps that were being sent. It was goodbye to her
plans for Christmas, but duty called and that was that.

She set off with the convoy on her 200 mile drive to Manchester
in the blackout, arriving at the height of the raid. Vera immediately
set out for one of the front line positions to serve refreshments to
firemen nearing exhaustion. Then back to the station to replenish
supplies and off again to a new spot. With the 'all clear' a weary
canteen van crew reported back to base, was given breakfast and

bedded down in a hostel. In mid-morning they were wakened and asked if they would help in the kitchen. 'There are so many reinforcing crews to feed that we can't cope.' So Vera and her comrades turned to and helped the kitchen staff with the rush. Back to bed after lunch for a short nap before the sirens went for the second night and a repeat performance.

The canteen van again set up for business right up with the battling firefighters amid exploding bombs and with others whistling down. From overhead came the menacing drone of enemy bombers cruising around. Blazing buildings crumbled and anti-aircraft guns contributed a fearful racket to the brain-numbing din. Ambulances collected the wounded, mortuary vans moved quietly around, their crews silhouetted against the flames, going about their grim task. Exhausted firemen reached for a cup of tea and a biscuit, still managing to exchange a joke with the canteen girls in spite of their discomfort; nerves on edge and with saturated uniform and under-clothing clinging to shivering bodies.

Came the dawn and the departure of the raiders; the London convoy was detailed to return home. Vera Linfield and her comrades made ready but just before their start, one of the canteen van crews was approached by an officer. 'Two London firemen from Islington were killed, last night. Would you take their bodies back to London?'

So the coffins were loaded into the canteen van and two rather subdued firewomen set out on the long drive back with their depressing cargo.

The ending of the second major attack on Manchester marked the beginning of an unofficial truce over Christmas. Word had reached the British Government from the German Embassy in Washington that attacks on Britain would be suspended provided the RAF also refrained from carrying out attacks on Germany. No bombing raids were carried out by either side from Christmas Day until Boxing Day when the RAF bombed airfields in France. The Germans retaliated with a sharp raid on London on 27 December which resulted in the death of 150 Londoners.

Two nights later came the city blitz, the worst night of the war so far as the city of London is concerned.

Shortly after 6.00 p.m. a large raiding force appeared over the centre of the metropolis to begin a bombing raid that was to last five hours. First came the heavy calibre bombs followed by showers of incendiaries.

St Paul's Cathedral, surrounded by large blocks of commercial and office buildings, was threatened by a large fire in Paternoster Square, practically adjoining the Cathedral's northern precinct. Further large fires were started in the Aldersgate/Moorgate area, in Queen Victoria Street and in the Minories, just north of Tower Bridge. Several bombs, off target, fell south of the river near Guy's Hospital and London Bridge railway station, starting a number of potentially serious fires but which were contained by the prompt action of the fire service.

In the early stages, ample water was available in the mains and good progress was made in stopping the spread of fire but, as more and more pumps were set in to hydrants, the water supply dwindled and was further reduced as heavy bombs fractured trunk mains. To make matters worse, the Thames was at an abnormally low tide, hampering the work of fireboat crews drawing water from the river. Fires began to jump the narrow alleys surrounding St Paul's and 'water shortage' reports became prominent on situation boards in city fire stations. Firewomen in control rooms all over the region were ordering pumps to various stations surrounding the 'square mile', from whence they would be directed to the nearest fire area. The enemy seemed bent on destruction by fire, dropping a phenomenal 300 incendiary bombs every minute throughout the raid. Fires spread with astonishing speed and it seemed that the whole city of London would become one huge conflagration.

Redcross Street Fire Station was at the centre of the inferno but the control room staff continued to maintain vital communication links with its satellite stations and with District Control. Said Firewoman Jean Savory, 'The firewomen at Redcross Street were very young. I was twenty, which was about average, our woman company officer was twenty-one. Station Officer Waterman, our Mobilising Officer, was a wonderful man, no panic or shouting, he just got on with the job and expected us to do the same. There were four girls on duty that night to operate the switchboard, take messages and enter them on the situation boards and keep the log up to date. We had direct lines to our five sub-stations as well as exchange lines.

'The evening had started in the usual way; the sirens went and we all reported to the control room. There was no reason to think this night would be different to any of the others. We started getting calls to small fires but no reports of anything big. At one stage I and another girl complained that we had been in the service since 1939 and never seen "a proper fire". The mobilising officer took us out to the street and pointed out several smallish jobs, with the Cripplegate Institute going up nicely in spite of a TL at work. The control room was on the ground floor but was heavily sandbagged up to the first floor so we saw nothing of what was going on outside. It soon became apparent that the small fires were spreading into a huge conflagration. The phones were working reasonably well and we had a call from our least favourite station officer. He was at the Guildhall and said, "he was burning history for the sake of a few pumps".

'Our mobilising officer told him he was lucky; "we were making history". But he went outside and ordered two pump's crews to drop what they were doing and go on to the Guildhall. After about half an hour we had another call. "The pumps had arrived but what was he to do about water; the mains were dry."

'Our mobilising officer replied, "line up the men and (with a look at our innocent young faces) tell them to spit on it!"

Firewoman Jean Savory in 1939, carrying her gas mask and steel helmet.
As a whole time firewoman she was paid £2 per week.

'The situation board was filled with addresses of fires and we were writing on the walls. Senior officers arrived and asked questions like, "What time is high tide at London Bridge."

'During the night, the Regional Fire Officer, Commander Firebrace came in with his deputy, Mr Sullivan. After hearing the fire situation they left to go to St Paul's. They had abandoned their car as the roads were impassable owing to heaps of debris or fires on both sides of the street.

'Our mobilising officer was wearing a very worried look. Sub station "V" had been abandoned and the firewomen had come to us. We were out of touch with our "X" station, the Wool Exchange, after the first hour. "Y" station, Bart's Close, called us to say they were surrounded by fire and were seeking a safer place. "Z" station, Baltic Street School, also surrounded by fire, was evacuated and the two firewomen walked through blazing streets to us. Before leaving, they had looked for their gate patrol man but he was nowhere to be seen; must have found a safe haven. Some time later, "Z" stations phone rang. As the station had been abandoned we were afraid to answer it, expecting to hear a ghostly voice. But it was the gate patrol man. "The whole place is going up in smoke and I must be the only person in the world. Have you any orders for me?"

'The senior officers had made their decision; we were to leave the station at once and make our way through a tunnel at the side of the Metropolitan Line but we were not sure if the exit was available. An off-duty sub officer arrived, found a lorry and, like a knight in shining armour, drove us away. It was not easy. Outside, the whole world was on fire and we were in the middle. The city roads were surfaced with wooden blocks covered in tar and blazing away; other roads were blocked with heaps of debris. Our driver spent more time reversing than going forward but, somehow, we found Bunhill Fields and the driver decided to cut through the ground of the Honourable Artillery Company's Barracks, where fire pumps were at work on a section of the building. The last message we had had from them was, "Fire spreading to the ammunition store." But we were not in the mood to tarry and eventually made it to our "U" station at Central Street School which we maintained for the rest of the night.'

Firewoman 'Nobby' Clark was detailed to take her canteen van to Ludgate Hill. Said Nobby: 'During training, we were told never to drive a vehicle over fire hose without ramps in position. This night, I drove along Victoria Embankment, intending to turn into New Bridge Street and so to Ludgate Hill. When I reached the ICI building on the corner, I found an absolute sea of fire hose covering all roads, like spilt spaghetti. Imagine my quandary! But I reckoned everyone was too busy to notice me so I gingerly drove on, crossing the ramps wherever they were in position and eventually reached Ludgate Hill where I opened up for business.'

Over in Headquarters Control, Lambeth, the mobilising staff had been ordering pumps from all parts of the region to the city. At the height of the raid, 2,000 pumps and their crews were within the city, firefighting and relaying water from emergency dams, canals, ponds and from the River Thames.

There had been frequent occasions during the past three months when the total resources of the region were absorbed by calls to fires within the Metropolitan area; neighbouring regions had been called upon to provide reinforcements. With this experience behind them, the men and women operating the control had become seasoned veterans, dealing smoothly and efficiently with each situation as it arose. Tonight, despite the obvious seriousness of the situation, there was the usual calm atmosphere. Said Firewoman Margaret White, 'I was seated at the table beside our duty mobilising officer, Station Officer Bishop. My job was to operate the peg board as he dictated. Presently, his telephone rang and he answered, "Station Officer Bishop." I saw his face change colour and he became quite

After a long, hard night under attack during which their quarters were wrecked, these London girls share a shake-down bed in the Control Room. Company Officer Margaret Davis relaxes in a chair while Basil Forrester, Mobilising Officer, inspects the peg board, used to mark the position of fire pumps.

pale. I heard him say, "We will, sir, we will," before replacing the receiver. He turned to me and asked, "Do you know who that was?" and before I could answer he continued, "That was the Prime Minister, Winston Churchill. He told me that we were to save St Paul's at all costs.'"

But there was nothing we could do about it. We had ordered all the appliances they had requested and it was now up to the lads on the spot. But we felt that they needed no encouragement to save St Paul's.

Earlier in the month, the Home Secretary had suggested to members of the War Cabinet that a Fire Watching scheme should be introduced, under which employees would be required to keep watch on their workplace during the hours the building would normally be left unattended, i.e. at nights and weekends. The stupendous damage caused by the raid of the 29–30 December lent urgency to the matter and, on 31 December, Mr Morrison announced the introduction of a compulsory Air Raids Precaution for men. So came into existence the Firebomb Fighters.

In January 1941, adverse weather conditions over the UK and the Continent curtailed the bomber offensive. However, on the night of 10–11 the enemy carried out simultaneous heavy raids on London and Manchester and significant raids on ports and industrial centres were made on ten other occasions during the month. On the night of 15–16, Derby experienced its heaviest raid of the war. Impossible flying weather during February, too, severely hampered German air activity. However, some operations were carried out, with Swansea under fire for three successive nights.

There was no let up for control room staff, however. For those in the target area, it was just another nerve-wracking ordeal, with the sound of explosions drawing nearer as the raid developed, with added anxiety for telephonists receiving messages from air raid wardens reporting incidents near their homes.

Away from the target area, control room staff watched the situation build up as calls for assistance began to flood in. Staff car drivers, DRs, canteen van crews, field telephone units, fire control van drivers were all alerted and convoys organised to provide assistance to the city under attack.

On 6 February, Hitler issued a directive for operations against the English war economy which began with a review of the effect of operations against England to date. He spoke of air and sea operations and speculated on the damage to shipping and port installations and to the effect on the armaments industry. He continued, 'The least effect of all, as far as we can see, had been made upon the morale and will to resist of the English people.' He spoke of England and the English but the will to resist remained firm throughout the United Kingdom.

No matter how tense had been the activity of the previous night, the routine checking and testing of fire appliances, equipment and all communications systems, was sacrosanct. Accordingly, Firewoman Marie Thompson was detailed to test individually all the street fire alarms in the district. Marie did not ride a bike so she set off on her three mile jaunt. About two hours later it was a weary firewoman that turned for home after testing the last of the posts, with still half

A corner of the Home Office Fire Control, a basement under 'The Rotunda' in Horseferry Road, Westminster. The fire situation throughout the country was monitored on the large board, kept up to date via direct telephone reports from the Regional Headquarters. The Control was responsible for mobilising inter-regional aid.

a mile to go. But relief was at hand. A turntable ladder, with an equally weary crew returning to Prince Regent Lane Fire Station after a hectic nights firefighting, pulled up alongside.

'C'm on, jump up,' called the driver. Said Marie, 'Quite apart from the welcome lift, it was a great thrill. I sat up beside the driver and drove in style back to the station. The lads at the back were all standing cheering, letting off steam with the relief of having come through unharmed after another night of near misses. To me, this outweighed all the unnerving experiences of the previous night and it remains a very happy memory.'

After her ordeal during the city blitz, Jean Savory returned to Redcross Street. Said Jean, 'Looking around the immediate streets, I wondered if a fire station was justified in such a devastated area. Great heaps of debris were all that remained of the tall office blocks that comprised Jewin Street and all the roads across to Aldersgate Street. St Giles' Church, just across the road from the fire station, was a burnt out shell; the fire station and Whitbread's Brewery seemed to be the only buildings standing intact as far as the eye could see. It seemed incredible that the fire station had escaped damage; the flames had licked its very walls. Most of our sub-stations had been destroyed and there was little for us firewomen to do, so it was no surprise when I was transferred to Clerkenwell fire station in 1941. It was there that I learned to drive.'

When Iris Greenslade was transferred to Redriffe Road School in the Surrey Commercial Dock area, she left one happy station for another.

'When the blitz started,' she said, 'the efficiency and comradeship existing between men and women was something never to be forgotten. All those hours spent on drills and exercises proved their worth over and over again.

'One night, our station was hit by a cluster of fire bombs and the firewomen's quarters across the school playground was set ablaze.

Fortunately, all the girls were at their posts and the watchroom was unaffected. But the station was rendered unfit for service and we were all transferred to other units. I found myself attached to Trundley's Road school where I experienced my most horrific night of the war.

'It was a night that found our station right in the centre of the bombers target area; the whistle of falling bombs and the thud of explosions seemed endless. All our appliances had been ordered out at the beginning of the raid and our fire situation boards were full of the addresses of unattended fires. We were booking in crews from other stations and sending them out to the addresses on our boards; everyone was at full stretch. I was answering a telephone when there came an almighty crash, a whoof and I was blown across the watchroom by the blast.

'When the dust had settled, a couple of us went to see what damage had been done. The firemen's quarters were a mass of rubble and the stairs leading to the roof had vanished. Our first thought was for Robbie, our roof watcher and we shouted to him. It was a minute before he answered, "I'm trapped," but we could not reach him and he had to wait for the return of one of our pumps before being released.

'We could see fires burning all around through the gaps in the walls and could hear screams and shouts. The ambulances came quickly and took away the worst of the injured and we took in some to await the return of the ambulances. Fortunately, we had water to cleanse wounds and I was thankful for my training in first aid. We were far too busy to think of ourselves, although I am sure that most of us had butterflies in our stomachs. Soon, the ambulances were back and took away the remainder of the casualties and we started to clear up the mess.

'It was then that the reaction set in. The blood on the floor set me vomiting and I found myself weeping for the brave young woman with a terrible thigh injury, less worried for herself than for her little boy with a bad back wound, both of whom were to die on that never to be forgotten night.

'I was off duty next morning and arrived home still feeling groggy, quite unaware that my uniform was in a terrible state. I knocked on the door and my mother rushed to open it. She stared at me as if she had seen a ghost, then flung her arms around me with a cry, "Oh, Iris, I thought you were dead." Apparently, our milkman had passed through Trundley's Road earlier and had seen the wrecked school. He told everyone, "The fire station is down; there's nothing left standing."

'So we wept together with joy that we'd both come safely through that dreadful night. I had a cup of tea and a long soak in the bath. Mum prepared a smashing meal and we sat down together to enjoy it.'

On Wednesday 16 April 1941, the *Luftwaffe* unleashed the heaviest attack yet made on Britain. Some 700 heavy bombers, escorted by long range fighter aircraft opened the attack on London shortly before 9.00 p.m. The enemy's concentration area covered the dock and industrial installations on the banks of the River Thames downstream from Tower Bridge. As the raid progressed the bombers ranged over most of the metropolitan boroughs and many hundreds of fires were started. Casualties were heavy, with 1,200 civilians killed and 2,200 seriously wounded. Direct hits on a number of public air raid shelters helped swell the total.

Section Leader Prettyjohn and Firewoman Margaret Fruin had reported that morning for duty at Cannon Street Fire Station in the heart of the city. Their station was within sight of St Paul's Cathedral and they had watched the fires creeping towards the Nation's Church on that memorable December night. Over the past eight months they had experienced intensive action and had become a highly competent team.

Firewoman Iris Grenslade, 1943.

Major F. W. Jackson, DSO, commanding the London Fire Brigade, receiving a cheque for £5,000 from the American Red Cross on behalf of the Fire Services Benevolent Fund. Fw. Margaret Fruin peeps over Major Jackson's shoulder.

Tonight, the action ranged heavily around them. Their station officer, Roy Craggs, had been ordered out with his appliances early in the raid and reinforcements were called for to deal with the many calls still waiting attention. The firewomen were glad to be busy; it diverted their thoughts from their own immediate danger as the fury of the attack ebbed and flowed.

Said Margaret Fruin, 'We had just booked in five reinforcing pumps when there came an almighty bang and a rush of wind which sent papers flying all over the control room. Our lights went out and all our phones went dead. Section Leader Prettyjohn and I groped our way to the stairs and managed to reach the engine room where everything was flattened. Bodies were lying all over the place and we did what we could to render first aid to the wounded. We then went into the street and saw the devastation. The wreckage of fire pumps lay amid great lumps of masonry, stones and glass from the tall buildings in Cannon Street and more bodies were lying in the roadway. We rendered what assistance we could and took the names of the conscious firemen then went on to our secondary control and reported what had happened.'

One would have thought that Margaret and the section leader had been out for a pleasant evening stroll, such was the matter-of-fact manner in which their story was related. But then, so many brave acts on the part of firewomen have been described by those involved in similar fashion.

Their conduct was brought to the attention of the Chief Commander who sent a report to the Home Secretary. Section Leader Prettyjohn was awarded the OBE and Firewoman Fruin, then just nineteen, received a Letter of Commendation for her action that night.

Firewoman Rose Sennett was on duty at Homerton Fire Station, East London. It had been a busy night and, said Rose, 'I was working on the switchboard when I took in a call to my own home. A parachute mine had exploded in the air above a shelter that was being used for homeless people. I don't know how many people were killed that night but I do know my home was wrecked. I sat in fear and trembling for some word of what had happened but had to wait till our pump returned. The station officer leaned over me as I sat entering up the Occurrence Book. "I've seen your family," he said, "and they're all right but your home has gone."

'If that book is still in existence, that page will be smudged with my tears.

'I was given permission to go home and began to run along the

Firemen damping down next morning outside Cannon Street fire station
following the parachute mine explosion. The battered towing vehicle and trailer
pump in the background are from 66U station, Clerkenwell.

Station Officer Roy Craggs stands beside his staff car
and relief driver the morning after the bombing.

street but remembered that I did not have my key. I ran back for
it but on reaching my home, found I did not have a door. But my
family was safe and nothing else mattered.'

Despatch rider Win Hunt had been ordered to collect some papers
from Dean's Yard, Westminster. Said Win, 'Near Buckingham Palace, I was stopped by a traffic policeman. He had followed me along
Birdcage Walk and told me I had exceeded the speed limit for the
Royal Parks. So I was summoned to appear at Bow Street Magistrate's
Court No. 1 and was fined ten shillings. I thought that was a bit
hard; not travelling all that fast and on a Sunday morning, too, with
only a few people about and there was a war on. Needless to say,
the gang at my station clubbed together and paid my fine.'

I wonder what 'not travelling all that fast' meant in miles per hour.
I have the impression that Win was not prone to dawdling and the

speed limit in the Royal Parks is only 20 mph. Nevertheless, that policeman might have followed Lord Nelson's example.

Up in Birmingham, District Officer Todd was visiting the training school in Moseley Road, Balsall Heath where a batch of new recruits was being introduced to the turntable ladder. Several of the newcomers were reluctant to volunteer to be 'shot up', whereupon the district officer turned to his driver; 'Doris, show them how it's done.'

'I'd seen it many times before,' said Doris Smith, 'but I'd never actually been up a turntable ladder. Nevertheless, I was

Despatch rider Win Hunt, pinched for speeding in Hyde Park!

ready to have a go; I put on my hook belt, climbed to the platform and hooked myself on. I gave the arm signal and up I went to the full extension. I had a marvellous view all over Balsall Heath but when the ladder began to sway in the wind I nearly passed out. The operator swung the head of the ladder round and began to lower it, much to my relief. When I descended there were a few red faces among the men, especially when District Officer Todd turned to them and said, "it takes a bit of nerve to mount that ladder."

'The result was a queue of recruits, waiting for a ride up the turntable ladder.'

With the coming of spring and improved flying weather the Germans stepped up their attacks on port installations, particularly those on Merseyside, Glasgow/Clydebank and the Bristol Channel. The enemy was using parachute mines and bombs of the heaviest calibre in increasing number. March, April and May saw devastating attacks on the major industrial and armament towns, often raided on two or more successive nights.

May 10–11 was the night of the full moon and the night chosen for the heaviest raid of the war. London was the target for over 500 bombers who deluged the city with more than 700 tonnes of high explosives and nearly 90,000 incendiaries. The raid began shortly after 11 p.m. in weather perfect for bombing. For six hours, the bombers selected their targets, creating severe and widespread damage. A number of public shelters were hit, contributing to the heavy casualties. Fifteen hundred civilians were killed, thirty-five of them firemen, with roughly the same number severely injured.

Firewoman Win Mercer was detailed to take her mobile kitchen to the East End to provide meals for firefighters who had been in action throughout the night. 'It was stewed steak and boiled potatoes for the main meal as we all set to, peeling spuds. The range had been lit and we soon had hot meals ready for serving. I had just handed a plate to a big fireman when a small boy, looking up at the kitchen counter, said, "Please, miss, could I have a dinner? We've been bombed out but I've got tuppence." The fireman glanced at me then offered the boy his plate. "E'yar, son."'

Said Win, 'I still cry whenever I think of it.'

A heavy raid was planned for Birmingham for the night of 16–17 May but darkness prevented recognition of the target and the main weight of the attack fell on Nuneaton.

During the period 7 December 1940 and 16 May 1941, the

Luftwaffe had inflicted severe damage on commercial and industrial areas. One million houses had been destroyed or severely damaged and 45,000 men, women and children had been killed. Fifty thousand had been severely injured.

The lull in the raids following 16 May was regarded with suspicion and apprehension by those in the target areas. What was Jerry up to? Where would he strike next? What new form of devilry was he planning to make us pay for a few nights respite? But as the raid-free nights continued, people relaxed. Beds were made upstairs and the opportunity of a good night's rest was taken by those who had been confined to their usually dark, damp, cold and uncomfortable shelters.

With the pause in enemy activity, life in the fire stations reverted to routine duties. Although it was a relief to be free from the threat of death from the sky, the intensity of events during the past eight months contrasted strikingly with the comparative dullness of the raid-free days and nights now being experienced.

In the control rooms, firewomen found time passing slowly. Said Bessie Butler, 'Even when our fire appliances had been out for days on end, we were kept busy passing and receiving messages to and from District Control and dealing with callers. Our watch was over before we realised it. We were tired out at the end of the day or night and fell asleep the moment our heads touched the pillow. But now the hours passed slowly and we began to devise games and diversions to relieve the boredom. Boredom! How we would have welcomed it a week or two ago!'

On 22 June, the reason for the lull in the bombing became clear, for on that day Hitler committed what Winston Churchill later described as one of the greatest blunders in history; he invaded Russia. People in high places knew what was coming but to most of us the news came as a great, and most welcome, surprise. Out of the blue came news that hard pressed Britain had acquired a powerful ally. The *Luftwaffe* now needed every ounce of its power and resources to take on the Russian Air Force. Britain, if only temporarily, was granted reprieve.

During the preceding eight months of the blitz, the population of Great Britain had been subjected to unprecedented violence and hardship. Firewomen were no different from others in this respect, except that they were expected to remain on duty for long hours, often in inadequately protected control rooms during punishing and prolonged air raids, whilst others were able to take shelter. Firewomen despatch riders, officers' car drivers, canteen van crews, field telephone crews, mobile control units and mobile kitchen crews were all required to go out into the streets in the course of duty at the height of enemy activity.

The foregoing pages tell the story of some of the experiences of firewomen under bombardment. Reading in simple words how firewoman 'A' drove her petrol van to the docks to bring fuel to the pumps working there, or of firewoman 'B' coming a cropper on her motor cycle and landing on her face in the roadway, cannot possibly convey the full trauma of these events. The effect on the nerves of those exposed to the strains and stresses of life in war-torn Britain must be considered when assessing individual and collective performances.

There was the fear of sudden death every time the sirens sounded; the threat of being shredded into mincemeat as a large bomb comes whistling down. The thump of a bomb exploding close at hand and the shock of the blow on the soles of the feet as the impact is transmitted through the ground. The fear of being engulfed in a cascade of falling brickwork as a building collapses under a direct hit.

The crash of glass following a near miss; doors flung off their hinges, plaster falling from collapsing ceilings and a cloud of stinking dust enveloping the entire room, blinding the eyes and filling the nostrils. Flesh pitted with tiny slivers of splintered glass in face and hands. The cries of injured comrades as others strove to collect their thoughts.

Next morning, some would go on leave to shop for the family, queuing for this or that commodity in short supply. A half pound of sausages off the ration from the butcher; a tin of Golden Syrup from the big grocers in the High Street or a few oranges on the 'green' ration book from the greengrocer. Then home, to find windows shattered and plaster dust all over, the electricity still cut off and water, if any, smelling and tasting strongly of chlorine.

It was a struggle to keep warm. The bitter wartime winters made harsher by fuel shortages, icy draughts blowing through gaps in the temporary window covering and the dismal sight of gas heaters turned full on, the miserable quarter inch long jets barely reaching the filaments.

Back on duty next morning for a tour of forty-eight hours after an uncomfortable night shivering in the shelter. The start of another day of unrelieved gloom, of monotonous meals that satisfied hunger but did nothing to lift morale. Depressing news from the fighting fronts; news of the sinking of merchant ships bringing desperately needed food and munitions of war as the heroes of the Merchant Navy ran the gauntlet of the U boat hunter packs. The continual anxiety for loved ones serving in the Forces overseas. Tears when the pump returns minus one or two of its crew, or fails to return at all.

It was not surprising, therefore, that the strain began to show. My driver, Firewoman Florrie Ball, a diminutive twenty year old, had driven me to many air raid incidents. She had lain in the gutter as a 'big one' whistled towards us, dusting herself down on rising with no apparent thought for her personal safety. Yet she was overcome with horror at the sight of a trolley bus full of homegoing workers mangled by blast from a flying bomb, and begged to be excused further exposure to incidents of this nature.

Her condition is known today as post Traumatic Stress Disorder; then, it came under the broad heading of shell shock. But, like so many firewomen she carried on, with a little sympathetic understanding, pushing her fears to the back of her mind.

It took great courage to stick it out in those depressing and fearful days and nights and many had to dig deep to find the vital spark. The marvellous camaraderie which existed in the service helped. Quite frequently, firewomen faced with emergency carried on beyond the line of duty. Expressing their motivation, the explanation was disarmingly simple: 'I just couldn't let the others down!'

There was the inevitable joker who could be relied upon to start things off, even if the jokes were a trifled forced at times. But the vast majority did stick it out, performing, with great credit, all the duties they had assumed on the outbreak of war.

With air attacks diminishing, the Minister of Home Security was able to review the organisation of the Fire Service. Articles criticising the service had appeared in the papers. Lady Astor, Member of Parliament for Plymouth, started it off with a letter to *The Times*. She complained that local firefighting organisations were totally inadequate to deal with thousands of incendiary bombs dropped simultaneously. She also criticised the Government's action, or rather, its inaction, particularly in the matter of water supplies for firefighting. Other influential voices were raised against the inadequacies of the service as revealed during operations in heavily bombed cities.

Mr Morrison lost no time in investigating these charges. He convened a meeting of his advisers at which every alternative to the existing organisation of the fire service was considered. After lengthy discussion, it was decided that the service should be nationalised. The danger of changing horses in mid stream was realised but it was felt that the risk should be accepted. Accordingly, on 13 May 1941, the Home Secretary conveyed his decision to the House of

Commons in the aftermath of London's heaviest raid of the war, as firemen were still grappling with smouldering ruins in the City. The recommendations were accepted almost unanimously. Legislation was rushed through and the Fire Services (Emergency Provisions) Act became law just seven days later. The National Fire Service came into being on 18 August 1941, just three months after the Act authorising its creation had become law.

CHAPTER FIVE

The Nationalisation
of the Fire Service

O N nationalisation, the decision had to be taken as to whether or not women should be employed on actual firefighting duties. In some fire forces, women's pump crews had been operating for some time. These women were extremely enthusiastic and anxious to continue but, after considerable discussion it was agreed that, as a general rule, active firefighting was not suitable for women, primarily on account of their being, for the most part, not physically strong enough for it. But it was realised that an elementary knowledge of firefighting might well prove valuable to firewomen who would generally be left alone at their stations during raids and might have to deal with a fire while the men were away on the fireground. Every encouragement was given to firewomen to take part in elementary fire drills and to learn how to operate a light pump. This training proved very popular among younger women and women's pumps crews were often featured in competitions, the crews taking part with enthusiasm and ability.

Recruiting for the NFS, for one reason or another, continued to be slow and energetic measures had to be taken to improve the situation. Gradually, women fire officers established and maintained good relations with local offices of the Ministry of Labour which resulted in steady improvement in the numbers recruited into the service. By the end of 1942 the establishment stood very near to the target figure of 30,000.

One of the innovations of the National Fire Service was the setting up of a Fire Service College. The former Ocean Hotel at Saltdean, near Brighton, was selected and the college opened its doors to students in the autumn of 1941.

With the rapid growth of the women's branch of the service, it became apparent that in order to meet the shortage of women officers, training on a national basis was an urgent necessity. Accordingly, the women's wing of the college opened in January 1942.

Originally, only one senior instructor was required but, as time went on and two or more courses were held concurrently, the staff was increased, finally consisting of the supervisor of women's studies, three senior instructors, three group officers and six assistant group officers.

The initial scale of uniform to be issued to whole time firewomen was laid down in October 1941. It comprised one cap, two tunics, two skirts or one skirt and one pair of trousers, one gaberdine overcoat and one cotton overall. For those employed on outdoor duties, additionally a pair of rubber boots and a pair of gauntlets. Women despatch riders received uniform according to their special needs. All personnel received a steel helmet and a service respirator.

The so-called forage cap was optional, available to firewomen at a charge of six shillings. From a mere male point of view, I thought they were much smarter than the standard 'ski' type cap, a view shared by many firewomen. Doris Smith, stationed at Moseley, Birmingham, wrote, 'We had very smart forage caps with a bright red flash across the front. When we took part in various parades, "Wings for Victory Weeks", "Salute the Soldier" etc., I always thought we stood out among the other contingents taking part. Before setting out, our instructor gave us a briefing. "Don't forget you are representing the Fire Service so march with pride; heads up, shoulders back, arms swinging naturally. Watch your step and dressing. Good luck."

One of the early courses for firewomen at the
Fire Service College, Brighton, September 1942.

'I remember the write ups in the daily papers and when *Pathe Gazette* filmed one of these parades I heard the commentator say over the loud speaker, "Here comes our firewomen, so smart with those red flashes standing out on their caps."'

The inauguration of the National Fire Service was accompanied by feverish activity designed to get the new force into shape without delay in order to face a possible resumption of heavy bombing attacks by the *Luftwaffe*.

The country was already divided into twelve civil defence regions and these were used to form the framework of the new organisation.

This is the much improved uniform for firewomen, modelled here by Peggy Essex of London Fire Brigade Control. Despite the more attractive uniform, many firewomen had to be threatened with imprisonment in the Tower before they would part with their precious clothing coupons!
The firewomen had a genuine grievance. Women in the Armed Forces not only received uniform and underwear free of coupons but were given an extra allowance of clothing coupons for their civilian dress. But the firewomen were a disciplined body; there was no mutiny!

A total of thirty-nine fire forces, six in Scotland and thirty-three in England and Wales, were apportioned between the regions according to the fire risk involved. A new hierarchy of ranks was created; standard uniform markings were adopted and a general move made towards the unification of the service. Appointments to the new ranks were made and, generally, a smooth transmission to the new order was achieved.

In view of the proved success of the employment of women in the fire service, it was decided to introduce them on a far wider scale and that they should no longer be regarded as an auxiliary force but, like the men, should become full members of the service. This decision to incorporate women into the Fire Service and give them the title Firewomen, did much to promote that pride of service which became characteristic of the women in the service.

At the time of nationalisation, the strength of whole time women stood at a little over 5,000 so that, although all those in the employ of local fire brigades were automatically transferred into the National Fire Service, it was necessary to commence immediately recruitment on a considerable scale if the new provisional establishment of 25,000 was to be reached. It was soon realised that this figure would prove inadequate, and by September 1942 the requirement had risen to nearly 30,000.

With the rapid expansion of the women's section, there was a call for more despatch riders and specialised training centres were set up. One of these was at the New Cross Speedway in South London, where the facilities available were ideal for the purpose. Skilled male motorcyclists were appointed instructors and many firewomen despatch riders received their initial training there.

In addition to fire service personnel, the centre also undertook the training of WRNs as motorcyclists. As a friendly gesture, the Admiralty Clothing Store presented a set of WRNS despatch rider uniform to firewomen attending the course for every WRNS trained.

This is the new officer's uniform, also modelled by AGO Essex.

Owing to the acute shortage of manpower, now growing steadily worse, it was decided also to extend the scope of duties upon which women might be employed, to include the categories of wireless operator, hose repairer, tailoress and mechanic. It was remarkable how quickly women wireless operators mastered the intricacies of their work. Their voices, generally, were found to be more suitable to broadcasting than those of men. Hose repairing is heavy and specialised work; this, also, was efficiently carried out by women who appeared to enjoy the work and take pride in maintaining a high standard. A bit rough on the hands, though.

So successfully did the tailoresses work that within a short space of time all repairs and alteration to uniform were undertaken by them. They did particularly good work in the early days of nationalisation when uniform was being issued in large quantities and many alterations were required.

With the lull in bombing following the opening of the Russian Front, the opportunity was taken to adjust certain procedures in conformity with the new NFS Organisation. Experienced control room staff at key fire stations were replaced by newcomers in order that they might obtain full operational experience. Accordingly, Firewoman Marjorie Watkins and some of her colleagues who had served at Stratford fire station throughout the blitz and, at the age of twenty/twenty-one had become seasoned veterans, were transferred to auxiliary fire stations.

'After the blitz,' said Marjorie, 'our transfer to Credon Road school was like a rest cure. We had lived on our nerves for eight months, often falling asleep at our posts when the "all clear" sounded after a long night of bombing, during which we had had to call upon all our reserves of strength, mental and physical, to keep going.

'Now, we were able to enjoy a full night's unbroken rest and settle down to our duties without the strain that we had been under. Our period of duty was unchanged, still forty-eight hours on and

The mixed No. 35 Area Agility ream march out to give a display on a bombed
site in the rear of St Paul's Cathedral on Bank Holiday Monday, 1943. These
shows were always very popular with the public and attracted large crowds. The
girls wore bright red dresses and white socks and shoes, with red laces. The teams
were trained by professional acrobats and their performances rivalled in skill
similar shows seen in pre-war music halls.

twenty-four hours off, and our seniors were devising new recreational
outlets. Alf Maloney, one of our firemen, had been an acrobat with
a professional theatrical troupe. Alf was keen on physical training
and undertook to teach any of us who were interested, the skills of
the acrobat. Several of the girls joined his class and I soon learned
to take a run at Alf and, in two quick steps, stand balanced on his
shoulders. But I was more attracted to the eurythmics group which
had been started in co-operation with the local Civil Defence Corps

Firewomen despatch riders were shown no favours. They were required to undergo the same rigorous training procedure as the men. This girl came to grief in the mud of the No. 36 Area Fire Force (north east London) motor cycle training ground. And she can still manage a smile!

girls. We became quite good as a team and gave a number of public shows which were well received.'

Although the fear of invasion had receded with Hitler's attack on Russia, it was still possible that he would make a 'do or die' attempt to land troops on our shores. As a nation, we must remain vigilant and the Ministry of Home Security saw to it that our collective guard was not lowered.

The Home Guard, composed largely of battle-hardened men who had served in World War I, regularly carried out exercises designed to protect strategically important buildings and installations; power stations, gas works, main line railway termini etc. The London Fire Brigade Headquarters building came within this category and an armed fireman guard had been posted at the entrance to the underground fire control since before the commencement of the blitz. All personnel were issued with official passes which had to be shown before the holder was allowed into the control. In due course it was the turn of the HQ building to be the target for an exercise.

A detachment of Canadian troops were the attackers; a party of Home Guardsmen were to defend the building.

Firewoman Peggy Essex shows her pass to the armed fireman guard at the entrance to the London Fire Control at Lambeth. The steel door was sealed to maintain a gas-proof atmosphere in the Control.

News of the exercise created great excitement among the control room girls who prayed that the attack would succeed so that they might be taken prisoner by the dashing Canadian boys. But it was not to be. The Home Guard repulsed the attackers, to wails of disappointment from the girls.

Said Kathy Ochiltree, 'After it was all over, our armed guard told us that he had been approached by two of the Canadians who gave him a packet of cigarettes and asked him to mark their uniforms so

that they might be classed, "Killed in action"—they were fed up
with the exercise.' Said Kathy, 'I wonder how they got on in France?
I'm sure the Germans would not have been so co-operative!'

A streamlined system of mobilising fire appliances had been devised
and the new method was adopted. 'Much of our time was taken
up in exercising and developing the new system,' said Majorie
Watkins; 'none of us knew if Jerry would return and give us another
pasting. But we continued to enjoy our leisure time. We formed a
women's pump drill team; others joined the drill squad and, at night
time, the boys taught us the mysteries of solo whist, bundle, misere,
solo etc. Some of the lads kept rabbits in a section of the school
yard to supplement their rations; they had the cheek to name their
does after the girls. So Lily, Rita, Thelma, Marjorie and the rest
kept producing baby bunnies; we couldn't make up our minds
whether we were being flattered or insulted. But that did not prevent
us from enjoying the rabbit stew and dumplings when that came
along.

'I must say I enjoyed it all and my education in life really did
expand during those short six months at Credon Road, and I was
still only twenty-one!'

With the falling off in enemy activity, officers were looking around
for competitions of all kinds to keep personnel occupied and to
maintain interest. District Officer Vigurs, the Commander of 'D'
Division, Gravelly Hill, Erdington, organised a women's pump crew
to compete in a competition among teams of firewomen from the
Midlands. Said Firewoman Marjorie Meath, 'I became a member of
our team and we used to cycle to a station at Sutton Coldfield for
instruction. It was hard work but we were given every encouragement by the men and became very confident as the time for the
competition drew near. The prize was a Cup; we set our hearts on
winning and, to cut a long story short, we did. The district officer
was delighted and we were paraded around the eleven stations on

A spectacular finale to a Display given by No. 35 Area Agility team.

our patch by the district officer and his deputy to show off our trophy.

'The Cup was filled at each station and we all made merry. After the fifth (or sixth or seventh, heavens knows which) I and another member of the crew felt distinctly squiffy. I mentioned this to our trainer, Company Officer Perry and he advised us to pretend to drink, next time, and this we did but the others kept imbibing. We got back to our station that evening decidedly the worse for wear and went straight to the dormitory.

'There was a row of double bunks and two single beds intended for visiting firewomen. Those who had continued to drink were given the single beds as they were too far gone to climb into the bunks.

The women who worked in administrative jobs rendered invaluable service. They were the unseen warriors; the backroom girls whose work kept the wheels turning. Typists, pay clerks, stores personnel, even mechanics helping to keep the pumps and towing vehicles in good order. Some, after a full day in the office, took a turn in the Control Room or turned out with a canteen van to relieve the hard-pressed regular girls. Some, to my personal knowledge, put their first aid training to pracitcal use in treating casualties in the vicinity of their Headquarters and took a hand in rescue work before the specialist squads arrived.

L. Fw. Ruth Glendinning, seen here pulling at No. 4 in the tug-o'-war team, was attached to No. 36 Area Fire Force Clothing store at Leytonstone. Said Ruth, 'Part of my job was to collect clothing coupons for uniform. The men paid up after a few threats but it was like asking the women to part with their teeth.' We were required to make returns of defaulters to the Ministry, who took action to recover outstanding coupons. We decided we needed a bit more muscle to extract clothing coupons from the girls so we took up tug-o'-war!

'For the life of me I just couldn't get into mine, it seemed so high, so my mate gave me a leg up just as I jumped and I flew right over the top of the bunk and landed flat on my back on the other side. We were screaming with laughter but the off-duty women, trying to sleep, were not amused. However, they grasped the situation and helped put us to bed. Fortunately, it was a quiet night and we slept through to awake, next morning, with splitting headaches and vowed, "Never again, Cup or no Cup."'

Following nationalisation there were a number of transfers of male officers from the outer London area to inner London stations and vice versa. Said Jean Savory, 'We were not happy at losing some of our popular officers who were replaced by "strangers". A new-comer to Clerkenwell station was a column officer from Finchley, Arnold Hope. Column Officer Hope had done nothing at all to upset us apart from the fact that he had arrived and our old, friendly guv'nors had departed. Somehow, he had gained the impression that we were an undisciplined crowd and he set out to correct this with "talkback" evenings which we christened "The Bob Hope hour". We were summoned to the recreation room at 8 p.m. one evening. The column officer opened the proceedings with phrases like "A happy ship is an efficient ship" and went into a long spiel at the end of which he enquired, "Any questions?"

'There was dead silence.

'The station officer had a go and the sub-officer put in his ha'porth without response. If he asked a question all he got was a grunt. After a while he gave up.

'When we had gone, the column officer asked if we were usually that surly.

"No," replied the sub. "But didn't you realise that Vera Lynn was on the wireless?"'

Fame came early to Doris Carslaw. She joined the NFS in Portsmouth as a trainee despatch rider on 1 December 1941.

Marjorie Meath with her Cup-winning pump's crew team,
pulling out all the stops during a practice run.

'My early training,' said Doris, 'was to learn the situation of all fire
stations and controls in the area. On 4 December, the duty despatch
rider drove through the main gate at Portsmouth Dockyard which
was immediately closed behind us. We were told that a VIP was
due to arrive and that we were to go to the fire station and stay
there.

'On arrival, all the firemen were lined up in front of the station
and the station officer told me to stand at the end of the line. Shortly
after, a magnificent black car flying the Royal Standard came along
and out stepped King George and Queen Elizabeth. The Queen
walked through the ranks of sailors and came straight over to speak
to me! She asked me about the air raids on Portsmouth and enquired
about my job.

'"And how long have you been in the NFS?" she asked.

'You can imagine how I felt when I told her, "Four days, ma'am."
She smiled sweetly then moved on to speak to our station officer.

'Later, I was transferred to control room duties and posted to St
Mary's Hospital, where the sub-divisional control occupied the
former workhouse.

'Someone at headquarters insisted on the segregation of the sexes
and we girls had to sit at a table on our own in the mess room; no
mingling with the men.

'It took nearly an Act of Parliament to get decent toilet facilities
for our own use. The leading firemen nearly rioted when we were
allocated their toilets and they had to share with the firemen.'

'Just before the blitz started the Fire Service was very unpopular
with the general public,' said Leading Firewoman Rose Sennett.
'All sorts of insults came our way but it was a very different story
after the blitz. No praise then was too great.

'Our men were very popular with the girls who passed our back
gate. The lads stood around, chatting up any who stayed to talk. It
was a very convenient place, for the trailer pumps were lined up
with their taxi-cab towing vehicles in the dark at the rear of the
yard and many a couple hopped into the back of a taxi when seeking
a bit of seclusion. But they soon came hopping out if a torch was
flashed about in the yard.

'One night, one of our firewomen spent the evening drinking
with an American soldier in a local pub. He kept giving her more
money than necessary to pay for drinks, but it was firmly in her
mind that she was on duty that night and she gave the excess back
to him before she left. She came into the station a trifle more than
tiddley and obviously unfit for duty but we put her to bed and
agreed to share her watch.

'Of course, we had a visit during the night from the AGO, the
first for a week; she wanted to know why I was on watch and she
took a bit of shaking off!'

Firewoman Jean Jones recalls being transferred to the Croydon No. 2 Station. 'We were given one of the firemen's cottages for our quarters and made ourselves very comfortable there. We hired an outside cleaning lady to do for us, each paying a proportion of her wages. She was very happy to clean our cottage and we were pleased to have her with us. This very satisfactory state of affairs continued for a few months but it all came to an end when the National Fire Service came into being.

'New officers sped down from London and we were taken over by the tiniest battleaxe you could ever imagine! She informed us that she was our new group officer and she had a formidable AGO to back her up. Out went the cleaning lady and we were issued with dungarees and scrubbing brushes. We were required to scrub the floors and light the fire in Madam's quarters. Life was never the same!

'But I have many happy memories of my service in the NFS. There was a great feeling of satisfaction in the knowledge that you were doing your bit to help the war effort. Very often we were frightened out of our lives when the bombs fell close and, later in the war when Croydon became known as "Fly Bomb Alley" and the doodlebugs were exploding all around us. One of the many things that stick in my mind is ordering one of our pumps to London. It never returned and I must have been one of the last to see those men alive.'

Of course, like in all services, there were romances; inevitable, I suppose, with wives evacuated and husbands away in the forces. We had several divorces and re-marriages.

With the opening of hostilities, the number of factories engaged in war work rapidly expanded. Firemen in highly industrialised areas had been trained to know the 'danger zones' on their station's ground but it was soon realised that firewomen, increasingly taking over the mobilising of appliances to fires, could not be expected to memorise all the names and addresses of high fire risk buildings and those engaged in work of national importance on their patch. Accordingly, a list of local 'Vital Points' was compiled with a copy of the list maintained in each control room. The main purpose of the vital point list was to ensure priority of the attendance of fire appliances to these special premises.

In 1943, I was appointed to the London Regional Inspectorate team whose job was to find and draw attention to any weakness in the general organisation of the thirty-six divisions within the region. Our team consisted of a column officer and two company officers (men) and two assistant group officers (women). We were inspecting a sub-divisional control in a West London fire force and one of the AGOs was quizzing an attractive young leading firewomen mobilising officer.

The leading firewoman was distinctly perky in her replies and, obviously, was a most competent mobilising officer. Having dealt with a number of routine matters, our AGO asked, 'And do you know all your Vital Points?'

'Oh, I do, Ma'am,' she piped up, with a sidelong glance at the inspecting column officer, 'indeed I do!'

It was suggested to our AGO that she revise the phrasing of her questioning on this subject.

Senior leading firewoman Joan Tankins was mobilising officer at No. 17 Fire Force HQ at Crete House, Bristol and, in 1943, was transferred to Weston-super-Mare. During her time there, Weston was home to firewomen from several northern areas under the colour scheme.

Said Joan 'in 1943 my fiancé came home on leave from India and we arranged to be married. I was one of the firewomen who borrowed a wedding dress donated by the Federation of American Women's Clubs to British firewomen.

'My dress was applied for by my group officer and when it arrived, was found to need cleaning. She and her staff stayed up nearly all night washing it in the bath; dried and ironed it and then invited

London Fire Brigade Headquarters received many famous visitors throughout the war. In this picture, taken in 1942, America's First Lady, Mrs Eleanor Roosevelt, is accompanied by the Under Secretary at the Home Office, Miss Ellen Wilkinson, affectionately known as 'wee Ellen'.

Miss Wilkinson was a staunch champion of women members of the Civil Defence Services with a special regard for firewomen. It was her graphic description of their courage and devotion to duty, when addressing American audiences, that led to the donation of wedding dresses for the use of women of the NFS.

Also in the picture are (far left) Mr Herbert Morrison MP, Home Secretary; Admiral Sir Edward Evans, Deputy Regional Commissioner and (far right) Sir Ernest Gowers, Regional Commissioner for No. 5 (London) Region.

me round to her house for an inspection and fitting, only three days before the ceremony.

'The dress was of fine corded silk with a lovely train. I shall never forget their kindness in making my day so wonderful, nor the American ladies for making it all possible.'

Mr and Mrs Tankins outside the church following their wedding.
The beer barrel created considerable comment among Mr Tankin's Army pals,
who refused to believe that it contained only water for firefighting!

Fifteen wedding dresses were donated for use by British firewomen brides. Photographs were sent of each dress, together with measurements to enable a choice to be made. It was stipulated that each application for the loan of a dress should be accompanied by a charge of 15 shillings to cover cost of postage and cleaning after use.

Following a visit to the United States by Miss Ellen Wilkinson, Under Secretary of State at the Home Office, an American lady donated a further two wedding dresses. She had been deeply impressed by Miss Wilkinson's graphic description of the courage and devotion to duty shown by British firewomen.

The severe rationing of clothing and high costs combined to render 'White Weddings' something of a rarity in those days of shortage. As the result of this kind and imaginative gesture on the part of those American ladies, the morale of at least 140 British firewomen brides received a powerful boost.

Elsie Drury lived in Lincoln. When her age group came along she was called up, together with five other members of her firm to join the NFS. This was a severe blow to her boss who, being informed of the loss of valuable members of his staff, reached for his bowler hat and rolled umbrella and sallied forth to the Labour Exchange, remarking to his secretary, 'They can't do this to me.'

He was back at the office within an hour, a very subdued man. He had discovered that they could do it, and insisted on doing it, to him.

Elsie reported to Police Headquarters, Session's House, to be enrolled in the NFS. The recruits were conducted down flights of stairs, originally leading to the cells but now converted into control rooms and offices.

Said Elsie: 'I was issued with a blue overall to wear over my civilian clothes and trained in control room duties, eventually becoming a mobilising officer. Lincoln was not considered to be in the higher category of target areas although, as the war progressed, we found ourselves receiving regular visits from the bombers. We had several ports close by, Boston, King's Lynn and Grimsby, all of them on the *Luftwaffe*'s visiting list. Our greatest risk, however, lay in the numerous RAF bomber airfields situated in Lincolnshire. A favourite trick of the Germans was to follow our bomber squadrons returning from a raid on Germany, creating chaos as our planes came in to land.

'One of our worst incidents was within a few miles of our HQ. Two of our bombers collided on take off; they were carrying a full load of bombs and the wreckage fell over a large area. One Lancaster crashed on farm buildings, starting widespread fires. Parties from the airfield were sent out to guard what remained of the aircraft and many of our pumps crews were busy firefighting. It was obviously going to be a prolonged operation and volunteers were called for prepare food and hot drinks. I and several of my comrades volunteered and airmen and firemen were very pleased to see us. Those who could came to the canteen van but there were others whose duty would not permit them to leave the wreckage so we filled large flasks with hot drinks and walked across fields to those remote positions. As we approached we came near a clump of trees and were simply horrified to see the shattered limbs of an airman caught up in the branches. It came as a great shock to us but we tried to put a brave face on it and carry on with what we were doing.

'Perhaps such memories would have remained more vivid in our minds if we had not taken every opportunity of enjoying ourselves and laughing as heartily as we could whenever we had the opportunity to relax. We revelled in our friendships and remember many happy times spent in the Fire Service, but were never able entirely to cast from our minds the memory of those who died.'

Firewomen were barred specifically from service in the River Thames Formation, but there were two sisters employed as civilian cooks aboard the training ship *Exmouth*, moored at Greenhithe.

Training ship *Exmouth* with auxiliary fireboats tied up alongside. The line dangling over the side was used to haul up bags of coal for the galley. When the Officer in Charge, Divisional Officer Ashton, had need to deliver a message to the troops involving nautical language, he ordered the galley doors to be closed. Said Fw. Widgery, 'We always knew when the lads were about to have a strip torn off. The DO was always careful not to sweat in front of us girls.'

The misses Widgery, employed by the Greater London Council, were seconded to the London Fire Brigade for the duration. The boy trainees had been withdrawn when *Exmouth* was taken over as a base for 'B' Division, River Thames Formation.

With the inauguration of the NFS, the cooks were required to join the new service and, for a time, were the only firewomen attached to the River Thames Formation. Later, they were joined by three more firewomen cooks who served in the formation throughout the war.

Said Firewoman Widgery, 'The complement of *Exmouth* was sixty men; forty on duty, twenty off. The galley was on the second deck and ran the full width of the ship, quite large. It had two large

Thousands of firewomen up and down the country took part in productive work
to help the war effort in many fields of activity. In this picture, firewomen are
working on parts for the Mosquito aircraft. Many letters were received by NFS
personnel from firms expressing appreciation for work carried out at short notice.
The following is typical: 'It would be no exaggeration to state that but for the
assistance you have given us we should have been well behind in completing a
really vital part for the fighting services and need not say more than this for you
to realise what that means at the present time.'

"Esse" cookers which burnt special small coal which was brought
alongside by a tug and hauled in sacks up the side of the ship; quite
a performance, especially in bad weather when the ship was rolling.
We had two "galley slaves", firemen who were detailed each day
to help in the kitchen.

'Five auxiliary fireboats were attached to *Exmouth*, one of which
was sunk by enemy action whilst firefighting off Shellhaven. We
had some exciting times when we were machine gunned by enemy

aircraft, and a few near misses from V1s and V2s later on. German aircraft regularly dropped mines in the Thames and naval mine-sweepers were constantly sweeping the river off our mooring.

'Later, we were transferred to Tilbury and the fireboat crews were housed ashore. Firewomen took over temporary buildings in the docks and remained there until the end of hostilities.'

The general standard of health among women members of the NFS, whilst not so poor as to cause actual alarm, was yet never so satisfactory as not to be an ever present major consideration. In the building of a new service during days when the primary object was to prepare as swiftly as possible against expected enemy attack, health, although regarded as an important contributor to efficiency, was a problem which had to take its relative place with those of training, general organisation and the many other matters of urgency which went towards the establishment of the women's branch. It was constantly under discussion and closely allied with the pressing question of accommodation, but it was not until training was pro-ceeding satisfactorily that time could be found to organise such contributory factors towards good health as fitness training, outdoor sports and mass radiography.

The main contributories towards the difficulties arising where the health of women was concerned were that, unlike the women in the Armed Forces, those in the Fire Service were not on continuous duty, with the result that many hours were spent in travelling to and from their homes, often under the most trying conditions. Secondly, the duties undertaken by the majority of the firewomen were performed indoors where ventilation certainly was not ideal and, thirdly, and perhaps most importantly, a very large proportion of firewomen, being married women, had domestic responsibilities in addition to their fire service duties, a fact which undoubtedly created a very severe strain on their state of health.

During a conference of Regional Women Fire Officers, the health of firewomen came under discussion. The women officers were not satisfied with the general standard but several factors, in the circumstances, were insurmountable. Control room work was performed in confined spaces; many of the firewomen were doing two jobs and they were, unlike members of the Armed Forces, living on civilian rations. It was agreed that the maintenance of sickness statistics would be extremely useful.

The later months of 1943 and early 1944 showed the highest peak of women absent due to sickness. At a meeting of the Service Council, held in July 1943, the Chief Woman Fire Officer reported that the health of firewomen was beginning to reflect the strain of four years of war.

The standard of health of the women of the National Fire Service, however, compared favourably with that prevailing among the three women's services, where sickness among the women was estimated to be twice as high as among the men. A committee set up to investigate the amenities and welfare in the three women's services reported, 'The overriding condition in wartime is the national need, and the exigencies of a country fighting for its life resulted in temporary conditions of real hardship for women volunteers.'

A great surprise for the planners of training schedules was the tremendous enthusiasm with which squad drill had been received by firewomen. In the early stages, 'square bashing' had been introduced for the traditional purposes of instilling discipline and to enable squads to be moved about in an orderly manner. Some hilarious stories describing firewomen's reaction to words of command evoked great amusement, especially among the men.

Many women were introduced to squad drill before they had been issued with uniform. Quite apart from the difficulty of performing an 'about turn' wearing high heeled shoes, they were put at an additional disadvantage by the thoughtlessness of instructors, who formed their squads on grassland. At this stage, many of the women did not know left from right and the command 'Left Turn' led to half the squad turning in the opposite direction to the others, whilst several fell when their high heels sank into the soft ground. With the coming of the universally maligned 'clumpy black shoes', however, and a spark of sanity in the mind of their instructors, the women quickly developed a taste for this new form of activity.

May (The Voice) Walters was a firewoman attached to Burdett Road fire station in the East End of London. As enthusiasm for squad drill soared, May discovered not only that she was able to grasp the intricacies of directing a squad of women on the march, but that she was endowed with a voice of such clarity and far-reaching range that she had no difficulty in projecting her orders across a large parade ground.

May practised hard and long under the guidance of Section-Leader Sydney Hole, a former drill instructor, until they were satisfied that their squad had reached a standard when they might consider bidding for the Regional Championship.

I never met May Walters but I knew her voice. As I sat in my office at Lambeth HQ in 1943, I heard her putting her squad through its paces at practice in the drill yard. Her voice floated up, penetrating the offices and bringing work to a halt as we flocked to the balconies to watch this slender young firewomen, a trifle over five feet tall, moving her squad around in a manner that would not have discredited the famous Regimental Sergeant Major 'Tibby' Brittain of the Coldstream Guards. The Regimental Sergeant Major was a massive man, six feet three and of proportionate build but I would say that May, pound for pound, outvoiced the mighty 'Tibby'.

Came the day of the final. Two Guards drill instructors from Chelsea barracks were invited to judge the competition; they sat at their table and marked the score sheets as the squads performed all the movements in the book. All had been well trained and marched

Lambeth, 23 July 1943. The victorious NFS Squad Drill team
about to receive the Challenge Cup from Admiral Sir Edward Evans.

confidently, but the judges must have been impressed with the
performance of the tiny drill instructor, never moving an inch from
her original position yet controlling her squad effortlessly from the
far side of the large yard, bringing it finally to a halt in the precise
centre of the drill yard.

There was no doubt about the result. May received a great ovation
from an enthusiastic crowd of firewomen, massed on the Lambeth
Headquarters balconies, as she marched out to receive the Challenge
Cup from its donor, Regional Commissioner Admiral Sir Edward
Evans.

From them on, squad drill became a craze and firewomen battled to secure a place in their divisional team. With growing confidence, the Regional Champions threw out a challenge to teams representing the WRNS, the ATS, the WAAF and any other women's team that fancied its chances.

Firewomen revelled in the exercises and took great pride in turning on a spectacular performance. And they had their fans; fellow women of the NFS, cheering on their favourites like followers of the football league teams.

Firewoman May Walters (left) and her friend, Edith Buck, parade in borrowed plumes. A bit of fun at Burdett Road Fire Station during the 'phoney war' period.

There were several squads in the London Region challenging for top honours. Irene Wood was a member of a team from West London that had been trained by a Royal Marines Officer.

'We had a number of successes which boosted our confidence,' said Irene, 'representing London in several big parades. But the sun did not always shine upon us. One important event was a match against the women of the WRNS, the ATS and the WAAF at Lambeth. We felt on top of the world, turning and wheeling to perfection; everyone said we'd "got it in the bag", but disaster overtook us. Our leading firewoman instructor suddenly had a fit of nerves or something and lost her voice completely, leaving us marching straight into a wall!

'We were devastated. We had worked so hard and now this. But after a time we felt so sorry for our poor leading firewoman; she never lived it down!'

But May and her East Enders continued to triumph.

CHAPTER SIX

The Baedeker Raids

IN the face of heavy air attacks on German cities and the growing intensity of the RAF raids in the spring of 1942, pressure in the German press for retaliation was mounting. On 28 March 1942, the RAF carried out heavy attacks on the German cities of Lubeck and Rostock causing severe damage. The anger in Germany created by these attacks led Hitler to sanction 'terror attacks of a retaliatory nature on British cities, carried out to achieve the greatest possible effect on civilian life.' The German press referred to the Baedeker Tourist Guide and spoke of the intention to mark off, as they were destroyed, each British city listed. So, the operations of the *Luftwaffe* became known, in England and in Germany, as the Baedeker Raids.

Although other towns and cities were included in the German targets, the main centres singled out for attack were the historic cities of Bath, Canterbury, Exeter, Norwich and York. With the possible exception of Bath, the war-time home of the Admiralty, all were locations noted more for their cultural associations than their military or industrial activities and all were only lightly defended.

Exeter was the first victim of the terror attacks. Raiders appeared over the city on the nights of 23 and 24 April. Bath came next, on the nights of 25 and 26 April. It was the turn of Norwich on the night of 27 April.

On 28 April the attack was switched to York, then back to Norwich on the night of 29 April. On 2 May it was the turn of Canterbury, on 3 May back to Exeter and, finally, a return visit to Canterbury on 6 May.

Raiding or no raiding, fire controls throughout the country continued to be manned; the threat of attack was ever present and the Service stood ready for action when called upon. In Exeter, Firewoman Doris Willis, then twenty-two, was on duty at station 'X', Posloe Road, when the sirens sounded. 'The first salvo of bombs dropped all around us,' said Doris. 'Almost at once our lights went out and all the telephone lines went dead, and there was I, the only firewoman on duty, sitting in utter darkness in an isolated control room. Rather than leave me there on my own, the officer in charge invited me to join our pumps crew.

'Fifty years on, I can see myself there, complete with tin hat and respirator and as nervous as a kitten, doing the best I could to help. We were surrounded by fires and I helped with a branch for a time. I was terrified but it was better than sitting by myself in a dark, useless control room, just listening to the bombs coming down.'

Firewoman Joyce Arthurton was attached to the headquarters fire station in Bethell Street, Norwich. She had been on leave on 28 April and, said Joyce, 'I well remember reporting for duty on the morning of the 29th and seeing the faces of the firemen who had been out all night fighting the fires, haggard and dusty, their uniforms covered in a grey film. Two had not returned from a fire in Oak Street; they had been trying to release some trapped horses when a bomb exploded nearby killing one of them and seriously injuring another. That night we had our second big raid and I remember the control room being filled with officers who had come with a convoy of pumps from London. Once the calls started to come in they all went out with their pumps.

'There were four firewomen on duty taking in calls and keeping the mobilising board up to date. We used a tag with a metal ring to mark the location of the pumps and I remember the tinkling noise the rings made as they rattled against the board when a bomb exploded nearby.

Firewomen at work in Canterbury Control Room. The possibility of a gas attack was taken very seriously and personnel were required to wear respirators at frequent intervals. The respirator for use by the telephonist is kept readily available. Emergency lighting in this control is provided by incandescent paraffin lamps suspended from the ceiling.

'I came off duty the following morning and came across a length of hose in Magdalen Street on my way home. I started to roll it up to avoid anyone tripping over it when I heard a woman's voice say, "Oh, thank goodness, the fire brigade is here," but it was only me rolling up a discarded length of hose. These poor people's house was on fire and we had no pump to send them.'

Accompanying the convoy sent from London to the aid of badly hit Norwich was a mobile kitchen, MK 72, driven by Firewoman

Elsie Maskell. Its purpose was to feed the London men and it carried all the necessary food and equipment. Five hundredweight of coal for the stove, one hundred gallons of water, four hundred plates, mugs, cutlery, pots and pans and, among other necessities, baking tins each able to make forty portions of Yorkshire pudding. Three firewomen cooks were there to prepare and cook the food, with assistance from the driver. 'I remember we were in Norwich for five days,' said Elsie. 'We had a stores van which carried our food supply and, in addition, all sorts of items considered necessary; spare hose, even a few cans of petrol for the pumps. We replenished our stocks of food, coal and water in Lowestoft to relieve the Norwich people; they had plenty of problems of their own.'

Firewomen Edith Gaunt and Joan Roberts were members of a Field Telephone Unit stationed in Morley, West Yorkshire. On the night of 28 April 1942 the Field Telephone Unit was ordered to York following the heavy raid on the city. The central telephone exchange had been put out of action and all telephone links cut. Said Edith, 'I remember seeing the whole place on fire and our first job was to link up the fire stations. During the dark hours we laid our wires in gutters running with water and filled with broken glass and debris and managed to get communications working. When daylight came we had to secure our wires in trees, up lamp posts, along the old city walls, wherever we could find a place to fix them. We laid over three miles of telephone wires in under two hours. All the time, the guns were firing and bombs were exploding.'

Joan was marooned on top of Skeldergate Bridge fixing her wires. 'The van moved on as I climbed up the bridge,' she said. 'I finished what I was doing but the van was busy and I was left standing there with nothing to do. People collected below and called up, asking me what I was doing up there; I told them I was waiting to be called for. And it was quite a wait until the van returned with the ladder and I came down. We stayed in York for a week until the

GPO was fully working again. Our vans carried ten miles of twin cable, sixteen telephone instruments and one mobile exchange which we operated from the van. We had all our equipment in use, that night.'

Whether Hitler would have continued with the Baedeker Raids had he not been busy preparing for the Russian Campaign is a matter for conjecture.

During the thirteen Baedeker raids, over 1,000 civilians were killed and 1,400 severely injured. Forty German aircraft were destroyed.

CHAPTER SEVEN

Scalded Cats

AT the beginning of 1943, the *Luftwaffe* began what came to be known variously as the Scalded Cat or Hit and Run raids in which small flights of fast, high flying aircraft roared over their targets, dropped their bombs and fled for home as quickly as possible. Although the weight of these attacks was far less than major cities had experienced during the autumn and winter of 1940–41, considerable damage and casualties resulted.

At that time, a new addition to the anti-aircraft defences was beginning to appear, a battery of sixty rockets, known as a 'Z' battery, grouped together and designed to be fired simultaneously. Since it was a secret weapon, the batteries were camouflaged and hidden in small groups of trees, etc., in parks and open spaces surrounding the main targets.

The 'Z' batteries were first used in London in early March 1943. They succeeded in frightening the life out of thousands of citizens, including myself, when the terrifying roar of the fire and the following, sustained s-w-eeee-s-h of the sixty rockets soaring into the sky, was heard for the first time.

It was the first firing of the 'Z' battery in Victoria Park, East London, that was responsible for one of the great tragedies of the war. Hundreds of people were descending into the uncompleted tube station at Bethnal Green after the sirens had sounded when the battery opened fire. There was a surge of people from the back; someone stumbled at the front and a great heap of bodies piled up on the stairs. By the time it was cleared, more than 170 had died in those few terrible minutes.

Farther east, on Wanstead Flats, another 'Z' battery had been set in a clump of trees alongside the Woodford Road.

It was along this road that a certain young firewoman drove the staff car from her base, the No. 36 Fire Force Headquarters, to the docks, a regular assignment. She was a lively, cheerful girl, full of fun and wont to express herself in basic English. Babs, we'll call her that, had driven an officer to the docks and was returning along Woodford Road with a message when, passing the trees, the battery was fired. A few minutes later, Babs reported to the control room. She slammed her tin hat on a table and informed all and sundry: 'I was passing the trees when that so-and-so gun went off. I swear the car jumped six feet in the air and I nearly had twins on the spot. Now, if you'll excuse me, I gotter go and change me knickers.'

Firewomen who attended courses at the NFS College at Saltdean in 1942–3 will remember the hit and run raids. German aircraft came in low, swooping over the coast in an effort to catch the defences napping. The first those in the college knew of an attack was the roar of an aircraft zooming over the coast; the rattle of machine guns followed by the thud of bombs and the scream of engines as the Nazi turned for home under full throttle. It was all over in a few moments.

Jerry did not always get away with it. I was at the college in February 1943 when the gunners on the cliffs scored a direct hit on a Dornier 217 which crashed in Saltdean.

A grim item of news, so commonplace at the time as to scarcely warrant the raising of an eyebrow, was the report that part of the aircraft bounced over a house in Holmbush Avenue and landed in the garden, depositing the headless body of a crew member within yards of the back doorstep!

Similar raids were taking place all along the south coast from Dover to Falmouth. Generally, they could be described as nuisance raids so far as actual damage was concerned, but some resulted in significant loss of life.

Seven people were killed in a hit and run raid on the outskirts of Bournemouth on the same day as the Salt-dean incident. Among the dead were three members of the NFS, Firewomen Sybil Young, Doris Lay and Daisy Kerley. All were returning from leave and were waiting for a bus to take them to their posts at Divisional Headquarters. The raider came roaring in over the rooftops, dropped his bombs and went streaking for home.

Firewoman Sybil Laura Young.

Doris Lay and Daisy Kerley came from Micheldever and Twyford respectively, two remote, small towns in the heart of the peaceful Hampshire countryside. With their comrade, Sybil Young, who lived on the outskirts of Bournemouth, they had been posted to Bournemouth on joining the NFS.

All the firewomen were buried in their home town with full Service Honours. Firewoman Young's funeral was attended by the Deputy Fire Force Commander and Divisional Officers; her coffin, draped with the Union Jack and carried by four firemen, was followed to the graveside by a large contingent of firewomen.

AGO Dorothy Twivey, from Sheffield, was one of the early

students at the Fire Service College at Brighton. Said Dorothy, 'We found the course hard work and enjoyed the rest at weekends. Our usual stroll was along the sea front for a drink in the pub at Rottingdean or Peacehaven. One Saturday, several of us took a bus ride into Brighton when, suddenly, a German aircraft came in low over the cliff and machine-gunned a block of flats, just across the road from where we were. The ack-ack gunners blazed away but he flew off fast; our driver put his foot down and roared into Brighton at about sixty miles an hour.

Assistant Group Officer
Dorothy Twivey, from Sheffield.

'The exclusive girls school, Roedean, about half a mile from the college, had been taken over as a convalescent home by St Dunstan's, a rehabilitation centre for soldiers blinded in action. There was also a contingent of wounded Canadian soldiers at Roedean, all dressed in hospital blue and recently returned from the Dieppe raid. They were in pretty bad shape and badly in need of cheering up. Their CO invited thirty firewomen to a social evening and we drew lots; I was one of the lucky ones.

'An instructor accompanied us as chaperon but we found the men were all walking-wounded or shell shocked and in no mood for socialising. We were disappointed but were so sorry for those men, so depressed and unable to relax. The evening was a flop and we were soon back in the college.

'I caught a heavy cold while at Brighton and had not shaken it off before returning home. I turned out one evening when the sirens sounded, without a voice and feeling very sorry for myself.

'An old fireman brought me a cup of very hot milk with a heavy sprinkling of pepper on top and stood over me while I drank it all. I don't know how I got through it but he kept saying, "drink it up—all of it," and it was clear that he was not going to depart until it was all gone. I was perspiring freely and my throat was burning but, in the morning, my voice had returned and my cold had gone!'

CHAPTER EIGHT

The Colour Scheme

DURING 1944 southern England, preparing for the Normandy invasion, was rapidly becoming a vast armed camp containing huge dumps of ammunition, petrol and miscellaneous stores, to say nothing of acres upon acres of parked vehicles. Quite apart from the anticipated massive enemy attacks, a considerable fire risk was accumulating and, to take care of this, National Fire Service cover was planned under the code name 'Colour Scheme'.

In August 1943, the scheme had been preceded by Exercise 'Harlequin' involving the movement of some 500 firewomen from the less vulnerable parts of the country to strategic points in the south. Valuable experience had been gained from Harlequin which was put to good use in planning for Colour Scheme. Briefly, the less vulnerable parts of the country were designated 'brown'. Any personnel transferred under the scheme from brown areas would not be replaced.

The 'green' areas remained static and any personnel transferred would be replaced. The 'blue' areas were the vulnerable south and south-east coastal areas covering the ports from which the invasion fleet would sail. These areas were to be heavily reinforced with operational fire crews and the necessary ancillary services. Some 2,000 firewomen were required to reinforce the controls covering these areas and the operation became, particularly for the women officers, one of the biggest jobs of the war years, since practically none of them was untouched by it in one way or another.

Women throughout the country received Colour Scheme with

enthusiasm. In the brown and green areas, women of all ranks were keen to be transferred whilst, in the blue areas, personnel were equally keen to anticipate their reception. Detailed instructions covering all aspects of the transfer of personnel were issued. Both operational and administrative women of practically every category were required for transfer and it was decided to move an adequate number of women officers into the reinforced areas, adhering to the policy of the women's branch, that the rank and file should be well officered. Specialists to be transferred included fitness training leaders, training school instructors and mobilising officers.

In the brown and green areas the reinforcing women were chosen with great care; general efficiency, health and age being taken into consideration by a committee comprising the Area Officer, the Chief Clerk and the Establishments Officer working in close collaboration in drawing up the lists to be submitted to the Fire Force Commander.

Women to be transferred were usually notified from a week to ten days before the event and were given the opportunity of appealing if they so desired. Those who accepted were given two days leave, returning to duty on the day before their departure. The need for secrecy was impressed upon them in security lectures.

The Chief of Fire Staff, Commander A.N.G. Firebrace, RN (Retd) relates in his book *Fire Service Memories* a conversation he had in Brighton fire control with a reinforcing firewoman. 'I asked her, innocently enough, from what town she had come. Her security training held and her reply came in the broadest of Lancashire dialect. "I can't tell thee; I was towd to say nowt about owt."'

Infinite trouble was taken to make their last few hours in their home region as happy as possible. Meals and light refreshment were provided and entertainment, usually a concert or dance, sometimes both, were provided. All journeys south were effected at night which invariably left several hours to be filled in between arrival and departure from the regional base.

A visitor to one of the regional bases of the brown areas would have found an air of suppressed excitement among the hundreds of men and women awaiting the signal for their departure. At that point, any inclination towards homesickness and loneliness among the firewomen was swamped for the time being in the activity of the moment; the farewell speeches by senior officers and the concert and dancing proving an excellent distraction. But a wail of despair arose from the girls as the music stopped and a contingent of men was called away to join their train to the south. SYDS was the departing shout; see you down south.

Firewomen Doris Smith was driver to Divisional Officer S.H. Todd, with Headquarters in Moseley, Birmingham. Doris volunteered to take part in Colour Scheme and was detailed to drive her divisional officer to their destination. 'After a long journey,' said Doris, 'we found ourselves in Southampton. I got lost in the dock area and stopped to ask my way just as a tank rolled down the gangway of a ship and crashed into the side of my car. No one was hurt but the car had to be towed away. I took over a car provided by the local fire area.

'My divisional officer and I were billeted in a large house in the middle of the New Forest. I shared a room fitted with three three-tiered bunks with six local firewomen. The room was so small that we could only get out of our bunks one at a time. But we managed. We were on continuous duty and if there was a Red Alert, my job was to drive the officers back to Southampton, where it was expected that the action would be. I was standing by one night when a German aircraft appeared overhead, caught by two searchlights. The guns opened up and the shrapnel came falling all around us. I could hear it pinging on my helmet and I tried to squeeze my shoulders in under the brim. There was a peculiar slapping noise and everyone went quiet but it was only my knees knocking in my man-size wellingtons! I was terrified, to say the least.

'There were dozens of camps situated in and around the New Forest, filled with troops, tanks, lorries and stores of all kinds. I saw large galvanised tanks, formerly used for static water storage but now filled with petrol for army transport. Everything was hush-hush with tight security everywhere. Immediately I stopped the car, soldiers threw camouflage nets over it and we had to crawl out underneath.

'The soldiers were confined to camp during the six weeks we were there. As I appeared to be the only firewoman around, I often wondered if, perhaps, I was the last woman they set eyes on or ever spoke to. We arrived back in Birmingham to the news that D-Day had arrived and I was so proud to think that our firemen and women had played an important part in this tremendous operation.'

For many of the firewomen, particularly those in their early twenties, this was their first parting of any duration from their homes. It is to their great credit that not only were they eager to be moved for duties in the danger zones but they did their best to hide the inevitable feeling of homesickness arising from the break with family and friends as well as the familiar surroundings and personnel of their home stations.

Firewoman 'Nobby' Clarke had been transferred to the Home Office drivers pool at Boreham Wood, Hertfordshire. One of the attractions of life as a pool driver was the variety of duties that came along. One day, drive a VIP from A to B; the next, ferry a fire towing vehicle about the country. Said Nobby, 'I once drove a dump truck of gravel from central London to Hampstead Heath but the job that gave me the fright of my life was when I was detailed to take an empty truck to Falkirk, near Glasgow. Here, I was to collect a load of iron kitchen ranges and deliver them to Tunbridge Wells for use by troops camped along the south coast preparing for the Normandy invasion. I had no hand in the loading but it became apparent on the way south that my truck was overloaded. It was sluggish to drive and I had trouble in controlling it on downhill

Home Office Transport Pool drivers arriving for duty at the Boreham Wood depot. From left to right: Nobby Clarke; Dorothy Biggs; Bunny Harvey; Pam Holland; and — Royle.

runs. Although I did all the right things it was as much as I could do to hold it but I persevered. When I was nearing Sevenoaks, I came to a long, downhill run that nearly ended in disaster. I was in bottom gear, footbrake hard on, clinging to the hand brake but the vehicle was not slowing and I began to wonder what I should do when the truck eventually took charge, as I felt it must. Then I remembered a roadside café where I had had a cup of tea on a previous run. It had a large open parking space at the end of which was an embankment. I remember thinking, if I can only reach it before the truck ran amok I would steer it across the parking area to the embankment and hoped that my path would be clear. It was, and I slowed enough so that when I reached the embankment there was only a slight bump which did no damage.

'I sat trembling in the seat for a few minutes then staggered over to the café for a cup of tea. When I had recovered my composure, I spoke to a lorry driver and told him of my ordeal. Thinking he might have some special trick to play in such circumstances I asked him if there was anything else I could do. His reply was simple. "Pray, girlie, pray."'

Firewoman Dorothy Myers joined up at Odsal Fire Station, Bradford, in 1941 when she was seventeen. 'I just couldn't wait for my eighteenth birthday so I could be enrolled full time,' said Dorothy. 'I volunteered for everything that came along; squad drill, pump competitions, the pantomime in aid of the Benevolent Fund and time simply flew during the first eighteen months. Then I volunteered for the Colour Scheme and when instructed to report, the time could not have been worse for me. I had received an invitation to go to Buckingham Palace to see my Royal Navy boyfriend receive the Distinguished Service Medal from HM King George VI on 29 February.

'We were told to be ready to move out from Bradford on 24 February but not told our destination. After dark, we were marched to Forster Square station to board a train, destination unknown. Some ten hours later we found ourselves deep in the heart of Kent. Three of us from the same area were sent to Dover Road Fire Station in Folkestone where I applied for and was granted two days leave to attend the Investiture.

'I hadn't been back in Folkestone long before I knew what I was there for; the days of squad drill, competitions and pantomimes were things of the past. No sooner did the All Clear sound than the sirens would go again and we were shelled day and night by the German batteries at Cap Gris Nez on the other side of the Channel.

'It seemed fate that I had been posted to Folkestone. One of my

Firewoman Dorothy Myers (later Mrs Dockray) and her fiancé outside Buckingham Palace after Mr Dockray had been decorated with the Distinguished Service Medal by King George VI. This was their last meeting before Mr Dockray was severely wounded at sea in June 1944.

officers received a telephone call a couple of weeks after D-Day. She was asked if anyone at the fire station knew a sailor by the name of Dockray; his ship had been shelled in the Channel and he had been badly wounded. He had been landed and taken to the County Hospital at Dover and the fire station telephone number was in his pay book. It was my boyfriend! I was relieved from duty and the station officer arranged for me to be taken to Dover. Both the hospital staff and the station personnel could not have been kinder; firewomen changed duties with me so I could visit every afternoon until he was transferred to the Royal Naval Hospital, Sherbourne.

'After the shelling

came the flying bombs. We were told that if the engine cut out there would be about ten seconds before the explosion, but it seemed like two hours to me as we waited for it to explode. In August, two of us were transferred to Ashford Fire Station and we simply loved it there. When the time came for us to return to Yorkshire in October, had it not been that my fiancé was being discharged from the Navy on medical grounds, I would have had reservations about leaving. Many tears were shed as our train steamed out and we left our Kentish friends for home.'

In several of the Blue Fire Forces, the area training schools were taken over as hostels. These were insufficient to accommodate all the incoming personnel and, eventually, 100 hostels for women were established. They were furnished as comfortably as possible with a view to making conditions home-like for the residents. On arrival, each firewoman was provided with a gaily coloured patchwork quilt, the gift of the Canadian Red Cross. This imaginative, human touch broke the dull uniformity of drab woollen blankets and was greatly appreciated.

Kathleen Timson was called up for National Service at the age of twenty-one in 1941. She was directed to Fire Headquarters in Leicester where she received training as a telephonist and mobilising officer. Transferred under the Colour Scheme, she found herself in the Essex town of Chelmsford.

'Shortly after I arrived,' said Kathleen, 'the doodlebugs made life dangerous and we often thought that any day may be our last on earth.

'Our control room adjoined the main fire station; on the other side were cattle pens, for Chelmsford is an ancient market town. One night there was a terrific explosion and we received several calls. My colleague had pulled down the bells and I rushed to the door to give the crews the address of the call. I was met by a large pig, probably startled by the bang, which had escaped from the pen into our control. I screamed and the pig screamed back. The firemen came running and firewomen, who had been sleeping in a room at the rear, dashed into the control in various stages of undress. For a moment it was pandemonium; men running, the pig running, semi-dressed firewomen running, grunts and squeals from the porker and naughty words from the firemen trying to get round him to reach the appliances.

'Somebody shooshed him out and he was last seen disappearing into the darkness. What happened to him, we never knew. We received several doodlebugs, that night, and had other things to think of than worry about that pig on the loose. I think he scared us more than the doodlebugs.

'Our leave days were very enjoyable. We had lots of service boyfriends but we rooted for the Americans. They were better paid than our boys and gave us presents unavailable or in short supply in our shops; nylons, chocolate, cigarettes. Looking back, I think we were very mercenary but we were young and many lived only for the day.

'Travelling was restricted to an area of ten miles from Chelmsford without an official pass. But that did not prevent me from an occasional trip to London to meet my American friends and go to the cinema. Sometimes, we were ushered into the American air raid shelters during a heavy V1 attack and passed the time playing pool and table tennis, plus a spot of jitter-bugging.

'It was pitiful returning to Liverpool Street station through London streets battered by the flying bombs, with poor people pushing perambulators containing a few articles they had been able to salvage from their bombed homes.

'On reaching Chelmsford, I kept a wary eye open for Army Redcaps, who had the power to inspect our passes but they seemed to be lenient with Fire Service personnel; much more vigilant where Army men and women were concerned.

'I was demobbed in 1945 after four years service with the NFS. I was rewarded with a months leave, with pay, and a gratuity amounting to £32. Oh, and a Defence Medal!'

In 1943 a new system of miniature mass radiography, sponsored by the Ministry of Health, was introduced for the benefit of various groups of war workers. Criticism, principally through the Fire Brigade's Union, to the effect that control room work, in particular, might be conducive to the development of tuberculosis among firewomen employed upon these duties, resulted in the Chief Woman Fire Officer suggesting to the department that facilities enabling firewomen to take part in the scheme would be of great value.

The Ministry of Health agreed to the proposal. The first Radiographical Unit was sent to Lancashire and the second, to London. Attendance for examination was purely voluntary but it was found that many firewomen did volunteer and, from the Fire Service point of view, the scheme was considered to be a most satisfactory inauguration.

The question whether or not it would be advisable to institute lectures in hygiene as a regular feature of service life arose early in 1943. At that period the fact that the women of the National Fire Service were not working under similar conditions as those of the three fighting services, who were serving away from their homes, influenced the decision that such lectures were unnecessary.

With the operation of the Colour Scheme, however, the matter was reconsidered in the light of the fact that large numbers of firewomen were serving away from their homes and, in many cases, were stationed in the vicinity of troop encampments. Accordingly, in April 1944, a request from the Regional Woman Officer, No. 12 Region, for permission to arrange for two lectures covering venereal disease and general hygiene, to be given during a fitness training course to a number of women officers, was approved on the

understanding that the lecture was given by a suitably qualified
person.

On the advice of the Principal Regional Medical Officer, a lecturer
from the Central Council for Health Education was provided. The
innovation proved so successful that, in the following May, the
Regional Woman Fire Officers of Regions 4, 6 and 7 were informed
of the department's agreement in principle to the giving of lectures
in these subjects to women officers and firewomen in cases where
it was considered that such lectures might be of benefit to personnel.

'It was a very cold February morning,' said Firewoman Gladys
Nixon, 'when a fire car called at my home at 5 a.m. to take me to
my station at Church Street, Luton, where our party was to embark
for our secret Colour Scheme rendezvous. Men and women from
other stations in No. 12 area were assembled, all with kit bag, steel
helmet and respirator and we boarded coaches with blacked out
windows. The journey seemed to last hours, we could not see where
we were and the driver was forbidden to tell us. Eventually, we
arrived at Colchester which had been heavily bombed the previous
night. After a short rest we boarded another coach to Ipswich, where
we spent a most uncomfortable night in a damp, cold shelter.
Condensation ran down the walls and some girls slept huddled
together two in a bunk to keep warm. Next morning, bowls of
cold water were placed in rows on trestle tables and we carried out
our ablutions alongside the men. We had been filled with excitement
on setting out on our journey to the coast but, twenty-four hours
later, our enthusiasm began to fade.

'After breakfast, we were told our final destination; most of our
party were to be attached to No. 13 Area Fire Force Headquarters
at Hethersett. The girls were billeted in several large houses in the
Norwich area and our spirits rose when we were shown our comfortable quarters after our miserable introduction to the Colour
Scheme. We quickly settled in and learned to live and work together.

Travel restrictions were in force and for four months we were not
allowed to travel home without an official permit. But we learned
to hitch hike and soon became expert at waving down military
vehicles. My first experience of this was when I hailed an American
army lorry. I climbed up beside the driver and a huge coloured
soldier and was most grateful for the lift as I had several miles to
travel. When they put me down at headquarters, I realised I had
been travelling with a lorry-load of coloured soldiers, and they
gave me a great cheer as they moved off. My senior officer sent for
me and asked why I should have chosen to ride with coloured
troops!'

Firewoman Marion Holt was a member of the control room staff
at No. 29 Fire Force Headquarters, Broughton, near Preston. Her
initial destination under the Colour Scheme was in the heart of
Hampshire. 'We enjoyed a few days rest in a lovely old house before
being sent to our action station at Newport, Isle of Wight,' said
Marion. 'We were given a length of unbleached cotton to make
ourselves sleeveless tunics for fitness training. Having hand-sewn the
tunics, we were told to soak them in bleach overnight. Alas, two
of our girls put them in undiluted bleach and when they lifted them
out they simply fell to pieces! Howls of laughter from the girls but
not from our officers! We put on our display before Miss Ellen
Wilkinson of the Home Office, who had come down from London
to see how we were settling in.

'I was due to be married on 6 May 1944 in Blackpool and on
28 April a directive was received notifying us that all ferries would
cease from 1 May. Sheer panic! The church, flowers, reception,
dresses, honeymoon etc, had all been arranged to coincide with my
fiancé's leave from the RAF.

'So I went to see my AGO and asked if I could work my few
days before leave at Portsmouth to enable me to travel to Blackpool
for my wedding. This was refused, so I took french leave on Sunday

This smiling group of part-time firewomen was attached to Hitchin Control, No. 12 Fire Force. Part-time members of the NFS gave generously of their services. After a hard day's work in office or factory there was not much fun in spending a broken night in a fire station. Neither was it easy for part timers to make their way through the blackout to their stations with an air raid in progress. This particular group took over the duties of the whole-time women during their absence on Colour Scheme.

30 April and arrived at my parents' home that evening. I knew I would be on a charge when I returned to the island and there was quite a to do. After I had been found guilty, the prosecuting officer came and told me I should have had more sympathetic treatment.

'We worked long hours at Newport, seventy-two on and twenty-four off. I must say that wherever I worked the sense of camaraderie was wonderful. We shared the joy of a letter from a loved one, finding something in short supply in a shop and grieving when there was bad news. Two of our girls had lost husbands firefighting during the Liverpool blitz. I have some wonderful memories of people and incidents connected with the fire service and look back on the good times, the friendships and the work we did during the war with great affection.'

Firewoman Dorothy Tree tells the story of her service during Colour Scheme. 'We heard that some of our unmarried girls were to be sent to the east coast to relieve hard pressed firewomen who had been under bombardment from the German guns across the Channel as well as air raids. A few weeks later, with another firewoman from Tooting, we found ourselves at a station in Tankerton. The leading firewoman who received us asked my name; Tree, I replied. "In that case I shall call you Twiggy," and that was my name all the time I was there. They were a nice, friendly lot and we got on very well together.

'My friend and I took a walk along the sea front during a short leave period, past a row of empty, dirty shops until we came to one still open, with rope-soled sandals on display in the window. The notice said "coupon free" and the price was cheap. Inside was an old lady, surprised and pleased to see us. I bought some for myself and friend and back in our common room, I got busy with some embroidery wool I had brought with me. The result was some very attractive slippers which aroused much interest from the other girls. Soon, the old lady's stock was bought up and I was kept busy teaching the others how to do the embroidery.

'In my private life, my stay on the east coast was a happy one. I had a young man soldier friend who was stationed on a gun site near Canterbury, and we were able to meet when our leave days coincided. We were married on 23 December and many of my NFS friends came along to support us.'

Firewoman Brenda Laight's home station was No. 24 Fire Force Headquarters, Birmingham. After the usual after-dark entrainment, Brenda found herself in Exeter where she was appointed to serve in the control at Danes Castle Fire Headquarters. 'From here,' said Brenda, 'we reinforced the City of Plymouth, during their heavy raids. We could see the flames from our control room and were very anxious until our crews returned home. In one raid on Plymouth we lost a turntable ladder and crew.

'I made some good friends in Exeter. At first, people were not too happy to accept us but, as we got to know each other, we became good friends. I was really happy as a firewomen; I had a satisfying job, one which only a war-time situation could provide. I made the most of it and, though I say it myself, I gave of my best. There were some outstanding memories. One day the turntable ladder was in the yard and I was invited to take a ride to the top. I jumped at the chance and it was a thrill of a lifetime. I had never been up so high and I have never forgotten that adventure.

'My stay in Exeter ended in late 1944 and I returned to my Birmingham station.'

Considering the youth of many of the firewomen and the pre-ponderance of troops in the area, their behaviour during off duty periods was exemplary. Even so, as a precautionary measure, a Minute was issued to the blue regions, suggesting that sensible talks might be given to the firewomen by their women officers, without inter-fering in any way with the former's personal freedom.

One interesting feature of the Colour Scheme was the way in which many of the firewomen, especially those who had never been away from home for any length of time, gradually developed a sense of responsibility and self reliance. The majority of them undoubtedly enjoyed the experience of visiting the blue regions, where many friendships were formed. Their appreciation of the efforts made by the personnel of the blue areas to make them feel at home was very great.

On 10 October 1944, a teleprinter message to all regions in England and Wales announced the starting of Colour Scheme in reverse. All personnel transferred under the scheme could be re-transferred to their original areas but those who desired to remain in the blue areas could be retained there and regarded as permanently attached.

The Colour Scheme had been highly successful. As far as the women were concerned, a great deal of valuable experience, both from service and personal aspects, was gained through it. Coming as it did after months of inactivity, the general effect of the operation was to raise morale immeasurably.

CHAPTER NINE

The V Weapons

T HOUSANDS of firemen and firewomen deployed around the south and south-eastern coast of England were roused, on the evening of 5 June and in the early hours of 6 June 1944, by intense activity and the movement of great armadas of ships and troops. The night air throbbed and vibrated with the roar of vast fleets of bomber and fighter aircraft, *en route* to soften up the enemy coastal defences.

The long awaited Invasion of Normandy had begun.

The whole country erupted with elation as the news broke; the final thrust towards victory had commenced! The local National Fire Service personnel, together with those transferred under the Colour Scheme, braced themselves for the expected heavy counter-attacks by the Germans. But the *Luftwaffe* was fully committed against the invading forces and had few resources available for operations against mainland Britain.

Scant news of the progress of the landings filtered through during the morning and the Official Bulletins were cautious. The initial joy in the hearts of some gave way to doubts as news of deteriorating weather off the beaches and of stiffening resistance by enemy forces was broadcast. But as the first and subsequent days passed, the news became more heartening; Allied troops had established and consolidated bridgeheads and were advancing deep into the Normandy countryside, driving the enemy forces before them. Jubilation spread throughout the war-weary population; there was great yearning for peace and now victory and the end of hostilities appeared to be in sight.

But the enemy was not yet done. There had long been rumours of yet another of Hitler's 'Secret Weapons' and, on 13 June, just one week after the Normandy landings, the first of the pilotless aircraft crashed and exploded on British soil. The German High Command that day had issued a communique, claiming that the new weapon heralded the arrival of the 'day of vengeance'. It was claimed that the whole of southern England was covered by a huge pall of smoke from the fires caused by what the Ministry of Home Security called 'pilotless aircraft'.

In fact, the German Communique was a typical piece of Nazi exaggeration. Four pilotless aircraft crossed the English coast during the early hours of the 13 June 1944; two exploded in the Kent countryside; another a Cuckfield in Sussex and the fourth, the only one to cause considerable damage and casualties, at Bethnal Green, London, where six people were killed and thirty seriously injured.

I had been informed of details of the new weapon early in December 1943. In order to meet the new threat, the London Region Fire Forces were to be reorganised and divided into two sections. The 'Home Divisions' would attend 'peacetime' fires and enemy action incidents on their own ground whilst the 'Task Divisions' would stand ready to support any heavily attacked city throughout the country.

Since it was known that the VI carried no incendiary device but was, in effect, a heavy high explosive bomb, the need would be for less firefighters but for more rescue personnel to excavate people buried in the ruins of buildings. Accordingly, firemen were given special training in rescue work. I was appointed to command No. 36 Fire Force 'C' Division Task Force based in Ilford and this was my post when the VI attack commenced.

On the night of the 15 June, the attack really got under way with the launch of some 200 VIs, all of them aimed at London. Seventy three found their target and eleven were shot down by anti-aircraft fire. The remainder exploded on the launching pads or crashed before reaching the coast due to technical faults.

From that day on the VIs, referred to by the general public as doodlebugs or buzz bombs, came flying over south east England and London at random times throughout the twenty-four hours. There was no mistaking the raucous note of the rocket engine; it could be heard approaching by those with sharp ears a minute or so before appearing overhead, giving sufficient warning to enable people to make a dash for the shelter. It was clear that the enemy was firing the bombs from several launching sites, for they could be seen approaching from different directions, sometimes merging in the sky over the capital.

The VI was a small monoplane constructed mainly of steel. It was 25 feet long with a wing span of 17 feet 6 inches, powered by a rocket engine and carrying a warhead of one ton. To watchers on the ground at night, the approaching VI first appeared as a red glow in the eastern or south-eastern sky, flying at an altitude of between 3,000 and 4,000 feet.

Passed on by one cluster of searchlights to another as it roared across the sky at 350 mph, it appeared as a small aircraft, the noise of its engine swelling to a harsh bark like a motor cycle engine with no silencer, saturating the entire atmosphere as it passed over. A long, bright red flame issued from its tail, giving the impression that it was a raiding aircraft set on fire by one of our night fighter planes.

But that impression was quickly dispelled as more and more appeared, sometimes flying in pairs or three abreast. Suddenly, the engine would cut out and there came an eerie silence as the aircraft dived to the ground, followed ten seconds later by an explosion with extremely powerful blast, devastating buildings over a wide area.

It is difficult to convey to the uninitiated the nervous tension experienced by those who found themselves in the path of a doodle-bug. The approaching racket brought terror to the stoutest of hearts;

the fear of frightful, sudden death or a long, lingering one pinned beneath tons of rubble as the building collapsed. All who heard it coming were convinced that the bomb would score a direct hit if the engine cut out. The urge of self preservation motivated many to mutter the prayer 'keep going; keep going!' even whilst realising that they were wishing destruction on others along the road.

They came by night and day. A single bomb followed by three flying abreast; no more for an hour; two hours; ten minutes. Their arrival was entirely unpredictable and there was no relaxation among the defence services.

Firewoman Gladys Birchmore was taking part in a mobility exercise in Hyde Park on Sunday 18 June. It was a fine, sunny morning; a pleasant change from the dull and windy weather of the past few weeks. Said Gladys 'There were lots of people walking in the park, that morning, when, shortly after eleven o'clock, the sound of an approaching doodlebug was heard. We all froze and searched the sky for sight of the beast.

'"There it is," someone shouted, pointing in the direction of St. James's Park. All heads immediately turned and I uttered a silent prayer that the engine would not cut out but it did. Instantly, it dived almost vertically to the ground, exploding behind banks of trees about half a mile from where we stood. A great column of smoke rose high into the sky and although there was a sense of great relief that we had escaped, we knew that some unfortunates must have been involved.

'Our exercise was terminated and we returned to our stations. Later, we learned that the Guards Chapel, Wellington Barracks had received a direct hit. Divine Service was in progress and the Chapel was full, a mixed congregation of military personnel and civilians. It turned out to be the worst incident of the V1 blitz. One hundred and twenty were killed and a similar number seriously injured.'

Firewomen on duty in controls in the target areas sat at their posts wearing steel helmets, some unable to resist cringing as a bomb came very close, the vibration rattling any loose object in the room; mobilising tokens hanging on hooks; a spoon standing in an empty cup. There came a visible and audible sigh as the horror passed over, signalling a brief period of relief until the arrival of the next.

Some control rooms were better protected than others but even from the more vulnerable, there were no reports of any desertion. The explosion that created considerable damage to the Control at Brompton Fire Station earlier in the blitz; shattering windows, bringing down the ceiling and tearing the door from its hinges, resulted in the suspension of operations for fifteen minutes, after which it was business as usual. The girls put off rinsing the dust from their hair until after the 'all clear', next morning. Similar tales came from Controls in other heavily bombed regions.

Special preparation were made for tracking the fall of V1s in built up areas. Each fire station had its drill tower which provided an excellent look-out over the surrounding rooftops. A table, fitted with a compass card and a swivel pointer mounted over the card for taking bearings, was provided on the top of each tower. The District Control had a large scale map of its area, superimposed with a compass card marking the site of each observation post. Each of these cards had a length of elastic cord, terminating with a drawing pin, suspended from its centre.

Upon sighting an explosion, the OP duty man or woman would use the swivel pointer to take a bearing, telephoning the reading to District Control.

'From OP No. 7. Explosion 65 degrees.'

In the control, a firewoman moved to compass card No. 7, stretching the elastic cord along the given bearing and pinning it to the edge of the map. Within seconds, other reports were coming in.

'From OP No. 2. Explosion 127 degrees.'

The cord from No. 2 was stretched across the map and pinned, the point of intersection of the elastic cords indicating the precise location.

The system was simple, fast and amazingly accurate.

Fire appliances were usually on the way within a minute. The normal initial attendance was a 'section' of five pumps, which could be increased by the officer-in-charge after assessing the damage.

Marie Thompson relates the story of her first glimpse of a doodlebug:

'My sister and I were going on duty at Prince Regent Lane Fire Station when suddenly this object came roaring across the sky, belching fire from its tail. My sister shouted "Get down" and I replied "I can't; I've got my new stockings on." They were a precious gift from my boyfriend in the Royal Navy (now my husband) and almost priceless in those days.

'My sister was not one to stand on ceremony; she just thumped me flat to the pavement, where we lay watching the doodlebug as it cut out and crashed with a terrific roar way in front of us. But we were OK and so were the stockings. And that was our first, but by no means our last, encounter with a doodlebug.'

The unpredictable arrival of doodlebugs in the skies over London and the south east inevitably led to oppressively long working hours for all members of the Service. Firewomen's standard hours of duty, like the firemen's, were forty-eight hours on and twenty-four hours off and many in the areas under attack were actively engaged during much of their period of duty. The officers' car drivers; canteen van crews; DRs etc., were under considerable pressure,. As one incident was cleared up another awaited attention. The heaviest attack came on 2 August 1944, when 316 doodlebugs were launched against London and the south east, an average of one every five minutes. My personal record was set in July 1944 when I attended sixteen VI incidents in a period of twenty hours.

On this particular day, my No. 2 driver was on leave which meant that her opposite number must remain on continuous duty, driving from one scene of carnage and destruction to another. Regular meals were out of the question; we just grabbed and bolted a sandwich and swallowed a cup of tea when and where we could.

One of the minor problems at these times was the need to find a loo, a problem that increased in urgency with the passage of time! A man could usually find a corner where he would be out of sight but it was harder for the girls.

Firewoman Niki Oakes was attached to Shoreditch fire station as driver to Assistant Fire Force Commander Ronnie Greene. Said Niki 'We had been out all day and there was no let up after dark. I drove Mr Greene from one incident to another without any chance to visit a loo. I was becoming desperate, so when the boss was out of sight I got out and wee'd behind the car. When he returned he saw the pool and thought the car was leaking petrol. He dipped his fingers in it and took a sniff but made no remark and, of course, I never let on.'

It was an extremely arduous time for all in the London area. My opposite number, DO Leslie Smith and I shared the calls in No. 36 Area C Division, our stints amounting to continuous duty. It was no less tough on our drivers. On leaving a job, I became expert in snatching forty winks in the back of the car *en route* to the next. On arrival, the driver would park the car in a convenient situation near the centre of the damage and sit ready to deal with any operational message that may come in over the radio.

It was in such a situation that Les arrived at the scene of a doodlebug at Gant's Hill. He had just come from another at Clayhall, Ilford and had been on the go for several hours. Realising that his driver, Firewoman Rose Bagnall, must be feeling the strain, he told her that she need not get out of the car. Said Rose 'I sat looking at all the damage and the rescues going on. It was a cold night and I began to shiver. Reaching over for a blanket, I wrapped myself up and leaned back comfortably in my seat. Unfortunately for me, the door was not properly shut and I fell out of the car.

'At that moment two dear old ARP Wardens were passing, carrying a stretcher. There was I, wrapped in a blanket and lying in the road, providentially delivered into the hands of two Wardens looking for a casualty!

'I tried hard to explain what had happened and heard one say to the other "She's delirious" I just could not believe what was going on; they placed me on the stretcher and stooped to lift it to take me to a First Aid post. As he bent over, the steel helmet of the man stooping above me came off and struck me across the bridge of my nose. That brought me to my senses and I jumped up off the stretcher, clutching my nose, and managed to convince them that, before meeting them, I was perfectly all right.

'Next morning, I had two black eyes and a badly swollen nose. I told my DO that I had bumped into a door in the blackout but, much later, I told him the true story.'

Although flying bombs continued to be aimed at Britain until the closing weeks of the war, the V1 blitz is generally reckoned to have lasted eighty days, from 13 June to 1 September. During that period over 8,000 missiles were launched at this country; more than 5,000 of them reached their target. The rest were destroyed, almost equally by the RAF and anti-aircraft gunfire. More than 2,300 exploded within the London Region.

The Allied armies were sweeping through Normandy, capturing V1 launching pads as they progressed towards Paris. Their success undoubtedly relieved the British mainland of much punishment which otherwise would have been inflicted. The large fall in the numbers of V1s reaching Britain and the rapid advance of the Allied Forces across Europe led the Government, in September, to announce that 'except, possibly, for a few last shots, the Battle of London is over.'

But Jerry had another card up his sleeve – the V2 rocket. As the V1s faded, the rockets took over. Like the V1s they were orientated towards London; unlike the V1s there was no effective defence against them. Fired from sites in North Holland, they climbed some seventy miles into the stratosphere and fell to earth at a speed estimated at 2,500 mph. A phenomenon, quickly noticed by those within range, was that after the explosion, the rocket could be heard coming with a sound like the approach of a fast train. It carried a warhead similar to that of the doodlebug but since it penetrated more deeply, the blast effect was not as widespread as that of the V1, although damage was greater in the immediate vicinity of the entry.

The first of the V2s to land in Britain fell at Chiswick, West London on 7 September 1944, closely followed by another in Epping Forest. Thirty-six rockets reached this country during the month of September, a very modest total compared to what we had been receiving during the height of the V1 blitz. But the numbers of firings were being stepped up. During the next month there were 100 and in November 150, including the worst incident of the entire V2 offensive. Woolworth's store in New Cross Road was packed with week-end shoppers on the 25th when a rocket struck at midday, killing 160 and seriously injuring about 100.

The advent of the new weapon created no fresh problems for the Fire Service. Search and rescue, with the occasional fire to deal with, continued to be the task confronting the first fire crews to arrive at the scene. In the control rooms, firewomen plotted incidents and despatched crews as they had been doing since the first V1s burst on the scene in mid-June. So far as the Service was concerned, the only difference between V1 and V2 was the lack of warning of approach of the latter. The first intimation of its presence was the roar of the explosion followed, in a second or two, by the sound of the rocket diving to earth.

Opinion varied as to 'preferences'.

'I don't like these 'ere rockets,' said a woman after she had experienced a near miss; 'I'd sooner 'ave the old buzz bombs; you can 'ear 'em coming!'

She was not to be permanently disappointed, for the occasional buzz bomb did arrive to scare the living daylight out of most of us. Many found the long drawn out tension of the approach of a V1 and the fear of the engine cutting out overhead to be the more stressful.

But Jerry was an impartial foe; he catered for all tastes. With his carefully planned launching sites for the V1s in Normandy snatched from him by the advancing Allied Armies, he took to firing Flying Bombs from specially adapted Heinkel Bombers, launching them over the North Sea. Both V1s and V2s now approached London from the north east; 'Fly Bomb Alley' was re-routed from Sussex and Kent to Norfolk, Suffolk and Essex.

The pool of women drivers at Lambeth Fire Headquarters was in revolt!

The girls had been given notice that they were to be transferred to Westminster School to make way for a party of firewomen from provincial cities, sent to London for duties in connection with the Colour Scheme. They complained that their cars would continue to be parked at the Newport Street garage. In the event of an emergency, drivers would have to run, at any hour of the day or night, from Dean's Yard; along Great College Street and Millbank; over Lambeth Bridge and through Old Paradise Street to the garage, a distance of nearly three quarters of a mile.

With London under constant flying bomb attack this was held to be unreasonable and would result in unacceptable delay when a car was required in an emergency. Despite an eloquent pleading of their case, the protest fell on deaf ears and a date for the move was set.

Thus were the seeds of revolution sown!

Said Muriel Nyman 'We went to the kitchen and each took a dinner plate, all twenty-one of us, and marched to the corridor outside the Group Officer's Office. There, we formed a circle and each, in turn, ceremoniously smashed her plate to the ground at her feet. Group Officer Gold opened her office door and was confronted by her entire driving pool, twenty-one grim faced women, standing amid a pile of shattered crockery.

"'Is anything wrong?" she enquired, mildly. "I thought I heard a noise" and retreated into her office without further comment. Which left us feeling a trifle flat,' observed Muriel. 'Our protest, apparently, achieved nothing and we had to move into our new quarters, as instructed.

'But we had demonstrated the depth of our feelings about the move and our protest probably caused the powers that be to think anew. Whatever the reason for the about turn, the order was rescinded and we were back in our old quarters at Whitgift House within a couple of days.'

CHAPTER TEN

The Queen's Review
of Firewomen

WITH the enemy on the run on all fronts and the prospect of total victory coming ever closer, the Government provided the greatest boost to morale the British public had received since news of the success of the Allied Forces in Europe; the blackout restrictions were to be lifted over most of Britain on 17 September 1944. The lights were coming on again!

Although East Anglia and the London Area continued to be the targets for V2 rockets and the occasional doodlebug, the planners were already contemplating the end of hostilities. There would be no further compulsion to carry out Fire Guard duties; the Home Guard was to stand down and there would be cuts in the Civil Defence Services. The time seemed opportune to consider means of paying tribute to those who had contributed so much to the defence of the Nation. Among items of a similar nature affecting other Services, a special event was planned to place on record the valuable contribution made by firewomen to the war effort.

Her Majesty the Queen graciously consented to Review a gathering of women drawn from Fire Forces in all parts of the country. Early in November 1944 detailed planning for the Review commenced. It was decided to hold the ceremony at the Lambeth Headquarters of the London Fire Brigade, where 700 firewomen, selected from those who had seen action in the face of the enemy, would be on parade.

Firewomen had taken up squad drill with great enthusiasm and skill and, with their comrades, who gave show-stopping performances as members of agility teams at 'Holidays at Home' displays and 'Salute the Soldier' and 'Wings for Victory' weeks, were selected to display their skills before Her Majesty. The Review would conclude with a march past of one thousand firewomen drawn from all parts of the country.

Contingents from outside London began to arrive on Saturday 2 December to be met and taken to appropriate hostels in the capital. Appliances that had been in action during air raids were driven to the hostels allocated to their respective Regions. On the following day they began a period of intensive rehearsal of the programme as set out in the order of proceedings.

Personnel were required to be at Lambeth ready to commence at 09.00. Canteen vans were there to provide tea and 'wads' to those taking part and mobile kitchens prepared and served a midday meal. Rehearsals continued until 17.00 when those engaged were dismissed to return to their hostel. Two further days of repetitive parading and marching and fitness training display brought a polish to the entire programme which finally satisfied the instructors. The women returned to their hostels weary after three days of intense preparation but with keen anticipation of the parade next day.

The great day dawned bright and clear, but bitterly cold.

Firewoman Joan Roberts, who had been under fire in York during the Baedeker attack in April 1942, was among those selected to attend the Review at Lambeth. Said Joan 'We were told we were going to London (but didn't know why). Four of the field telephone unit crew travelled down by train whilst Gertie, our driver, drove the van to our hostel at Woodford Green, where we finished up in a college. On the first night we were there Jerry paid us a visit and we woke up to the siren and found ourselves surrounded by broken glass. The London people were marvellous to us; their attitude was

Firewomen parade in London Headquarters yard for inspection by Her Majesty
Queen Elizabeth and The Princess Elizabeth, 6 December 1944.

fantastic and they gave us a wonderful week, just like a holiday until
Jerry dropped in. It made us realise what the Londoners went
through; far worse than anything we had to put up with in Yorkshire.
We had to spit and polish up the van and keep our kit in tip top
order. On the day of the Review we set out for Lambeth and what
a marvellous sight awaited us. The balconies were packed with
firewomen and we lined up beside our van. Other appliances took
their places with their crews until the whole yard was packed with
firewomen and equipment on parade, all lined up in perfect order.
Along came a beautiful black car and out stepped the Home Secretary,

The Queen chats to the crew of a Field Telephone Unit from West Yorkshire at the Lambeth Review. This is the crew who helped restore the telephone system in York after its destruction during an air-raid in 1942.

Mr Herbert Morrison. Then came another shiny black car and there was the Queen and Princess Elizabeth (our present Queen).

'After a while, they came across to us and the Queen asked Gertie if the attacks had been very concentrated. She congratulated us on a job well done; a wonderful moment for us all and one I shall never forget.'

After inspecting senior women officers and other ranks on parade, the Royal Party moved on to the Headquarters Control Room whilst the drill yard was prepared for the display. Assistant Group Officer Margaret Harvey, who had been attached to HQ Control since early 1939 and who had been on duty throughout the blitz and the V weapon attacks, wrote: 'It was an all-woman ceremony, from the control room staff to the smart women despatch riders in their bright yellow gauntlets who acted as escort to the Royal Party. The Yard was a picture, with lines of firewomen parading as immaculately as Guardsmen. The appliances, with their crews standing in front, literally sparkled and the squad drill and agility teams put on an impeccable display.

As for us in the Control Room, it was a marvellous moment when the Queen and Princess Elizabeth came in and spoke to members of the staff. Altogether, a splendid, exciting event which went without a hitch and with never a male in sight!'

Her Majesty then addressed the assembly:

When I say I am very glad indeed to be here with you today, it is no empty form of words.

I believe strongly that, when future generations look back on this most terrible War, they will recognise as one of its chief features the degree to which women were actively engaged in it.

I do not think it is any form of exaggeration to say that, in this country at any rate, the War could not be won without their help. This is a thought which gives me pride as a woman; it also gives me something more valuable than pride – and that is hope. For the full understanding by women, as well as by men, of the real significance of War, and of how vital it is to be always prepared against it must help to make its future prevention more likely. It may well be, then, that all we women have endured in this War may, indirectly, save our children and grandchildren from another.

That is one reason why it has given me real pleasure to meet, and to talk to, you who represent the National Fire Service and the other Civil Defence Services.

British women have won laurels in many fields, but nowhere have they played a more distinguished and courageous part than in the many spheres of activity that go to make up Civil Defence here at home.

In the Civil Defence Service there are women of all ages and of all walks of life, for it represents in its richness and variety the whole of our national community. They number some three millions in all, of whom I have myself seen in their almost infinite variety of duties — the Women Police, regular and auxiliary, The National Fire Service, The Wardens, the Staffs of Report and Control Rooms, the Ambulance and First Aid Services, the Fire Guard, the Rest Centre Service and the many branches of the Women's Voluntary Services.

All have shown the highest qualities of steadfastness, courage and resource, and that they have proved themselves in action and in the face of acute dangers is shown by the imposing list of Honours which the King has awarded them.

The second feature I consider so striking is this. Many of you, like the sailors, soldiers and airmen and their related women services, have given up your peacetime callings to devote all your time to war work, and the way you have done it, while often still carrying on your own homes, is beyond all praise.

But the overwhelming majority have been volunteers rendering part-time service. At the end of a day's work in a factory, or after a tiring day in the home confronted with all the difficulties of wartime home management, you have reported for duty. Despite the many calls on your time and on your energies — the particularly trying demands which fall upon the housewife — you have never failed in your work. You have driven vehicles while bombs were falling; you have put out incendiary bombs; you have brought succour and help to those who have suffered from the attacks of the enemy. You women of Civil Defence have inscribed you names indelibly on the national roll of honour.

The course of the War has, with the help of Almighty God, now changed for the better and we hope we can see the end in sight. The need for your services may be, in consequence, less than it was, and the calls of Civil Defence upon your time and energy may not be so strong. For some of you the time of active service may happily be past; others, in certain districts are still, I fear, working just as hard as ever, but we must never, any one of us, for one moment relax our efforts until the War is won.

To all of you I want say, in the name of the country which you
have served, and are serving so gallantly; – Thank you for a difficult
job magnificently done.

The Review concluded with a march past of one thousand
firewomen, drawn from all parts of the country and marching as a
single unit. The Chief of the Fire Staff, Commander A. N. G.
Firebrace CBE and Lady Betty Cuthbert CBE, Chief Woman Fire
Officer, undoubtedly experienced a feeling of immense pride as they
watched.

Following the departure of the Royal Guests tea was served, after
which the London girls returned to their stations. Those from outer
London were given tickets for a cinema show and conducted to and
from by coach. The newsreel cameramen had been present at the
Review and their first rushes were shown at the evening performances. To their great delight, the girls were able to see themselves
on the screen, to finish off a wonderful day.

Next morning, it was back home with a stack of marvellous stories
of how they had travelled to London to visit the Queen.

Firewoman Peggy Muirhead was driver to a succession of Divisional Officers operating from Euston and Clerkenwell fire stations.
She had served in Central London throughout the blitz and enjoyed
nothing more than backing up a fireman, struggling single handed
with a branch, in the most uncomfortable and hazardous conditions.

Peggy had wheedled, cajoled or, possibly, purloined a fireman's
tunic (I never asked!) to fit her sturdy frame; she wore it on calls
during the freezing nights of the first quarter of 1945, as she drove
me to V1 or V2 incidents in the Central London area.

With the approach of the end of the war, Peggy applied to join
UNRRA, a United Nations Organisation for the Relief and Rehabilitation of Europe. She explained that her brother, Sergeant Air
Gunner Montague Edwards, had been reported missing on an operational flight over Germany in 1943. Her plan was that once in

The run-up to Christmas saw the personnel at many fire stations (this one is at Homerton, East London) busy making toys in their spare time for children in hospitals. The men concentrated on wooden items, while the girls sewed and knitted soft toys. They used off-cuts of wood and paint contributed by local factories, together with material trimmings and ends of wool.

Europe, her efforts to trace him would be more positive than if conducted from this country. My impression was that if information was to be gathered concerning the whereabouts of Sgt. Edwards, Peggy was just the person to dig it out.

The last I heard was that her exhaustive enquiries and travelling had led to her to Meeuwin, a Dutch village, where a Halifax bomber of the RAF had crashed and the crew taken prisoner. Three of them had been identified as members of her brother's crew but there was no clue as to the fate of Sgt. Edwards.

I do hope Peggy succeeded in tracing her brother. The single-mindedness and perseverance she had so ably demonstrated during her service in the National Fire Service and, I am sure, in Holland, were deserving of their reward.

The enemy maintained his V weapon offensive against London throughout the closing months of the year. One hundred and fifty V2s fell on London and the south east in November and a further 130 during December.

During this period, the recently captured Port of Antwerp was paralysed by unceasing bombardment with a mixture of V1s and V2s, mounted by the Germans in an effort to deny the Allied Forces the use of the port's facilities. During the last ten days of November, twenty V weapons were exploding in the Province of Antwerp daily. These, almost certainly, would otherwise have been aimed at London.

On 16 December the German Army under von Rundstedt launched a full scale offensive against the US First Army in the Ardennes. It was the final throw by the enemy in a bid to split the Allied Forces and, in the early days, it met with spectacular success. During the first four days, aided by weather which prevented the

---

The picture opposite was taken in the centre of Antwerp shortly after a V weapon explosion. It would not have been passed by a British censor but it is typical of a London street scene during the nine months of the V weapon blitz.

NFS personnel were at the scene within minutes of an explosion, unwilling witnesses of the full horror; the mutilated bodies and all the associated scenes and sickening smells. To firemen and women, it always seemed more tragic when children were among the casualties, whilst the unrestrained grief of the bereaved brought tears to the eyes of many.

Not all were affected to the same degree. One of my fiewomen drivers appeared to be quite unmoved by scenes that others found deeply distressing. She never spoke to me of her inner feelings; perhaps, like so many, she suffered in mind and shed her tears in the silence of the night.

Allies from utilising their overwhelming air superiority, the German Armies had advanced some twenty-five miles towards the Belgian coast. Then the skies cleared, allowing the mighty Allied air fleets to pound the enemy armour. The advance was halted, then turned back.

The British people, understandably, had become complacent. The news had been of the enemy retreating on all fronts. Street lighting had been restored and 7,000 members of the Home Guard had paraded before the King in Hyde Park before being stood down. The horizon was golden and optimism flourished throughout the land; the end of the war was in sight!

It was no wonder that news of the German resurgence came as a great shock, for most people thought that it was all over bar the shouting. They had been preparing for what they anticipated would be the last Christmas of the war. Those living in the major northern cities had enjoyed freedom from bombing since August 1942; they regarded themselves as being beyond the range of doodlebugs and rockets.

But, in the sixty minutes between 5.30 and 6.30 on the morning of Christmas Eve, there came a rude and totally unexpected awakening. Forty specially adapted Heinkel 111 bombers, each carrying a doodlebug suspended beneath it's fuselage, flew from their bases in north-west Germany towards the Lincolnshire coast. When about 40 miles off Skegness, the doodlebugs were launched, targeted on Manchester. Thirty-one of the missiles crossed the coast, about half of them falling in the target area. The others were spread over the counties of Yorkshire; Cheshire; Derbyshire; Lincolnshire; Nottinghamshire; Shropshire and County Durham. It was a totally futile effort on the part of the Nazis which had not the slightest military bearing on the German war effort or did anything to lighten the hammer blows now being rained on the Third Reich.

Hitler's avowed aim had been vengeance on the British people and, one supposes, the death of forty-two civilians and the serious injury inflicted on fifty others, can only have brought him some personal satisfaction.

A detachment of firewomen, 'every button on duty', march smartly under the slightly war-battered portico of the Rialto Cinema in Leicester Square, London. They let their hair down later when pictures of the Review appeared on the screen.

CHAPTER ELEVEN

The end in sight

THERE were no 'presents' from the Nazis on Christmas Day 1944 but the V2 attack was resumed on Boxing Day and continued thereafter without let-up. In January 1945, 223 missiles fell on London and its environs; 243 in February and 228 in March. Three of these, at McKenzie Road, Holloway; Smithfield Market in the City and Hughes Mansions, Vallance Road, Stepney, together resulted in the loss of 300 civilian lives.

The short-lived success of the German drive through the Ardennes had been reversed and the enemy, again, was in full retreat on all fronts. An increasing number of deserting *Luftwaffe* crews were landing their aircraft on British airfields and thousands of enemy troops were laying down their arms. The news from the fighting fronts was such that it seemed that total victory could not long be delayed; Germany was being pounded to dust. But it was hard for those at the receiving end of the rocket salvoes to feel jubilation at the news. Victory, for them, could not come quickly enough to bring to an end the strain of anticipating a massive explosion some-where in the Region at intervals of 2–3 hours, day and night; every day and every night, for weeks on end.

Many London firewomen considered the period from 15 June 1944, when the first heavy attack by V1s began, until the end of March 1945, when the last of the V2 rockets exploded at Orpington, Kent, to have been nine long months of unremitting stress and strain; quite the most intense of the whole of the war. And that was my opinion, too.

This vast crater resulted from a rocket on the Smithfield market in March 1945.
Firemen were at work within minutes of the explosion, searching for victims
buried in the rubble. The loose heap of debris, upper left, was unsafe but work
was allowed to continue following the recovery of a body.
More than 100 died here.

Banner headlines in the newspapers proclaimed 'Wholesale destruction of enemy towns'; 'Allied troops cross the Rhine'; 'New
Russian advance into the heart of the Reich'; 'Cologne Cathedral
stands amid the ruins'.

'Good' was our first reaction to these news items. We who had
assisted in digging out of bomb rubble the mutilated bodies of our
fellow citizens and seen tough firemen with tears rolling down their
cheeks as they retrieved the body of a child, had little pity for the

German people. We told our neighbours, 'Now they're getting a taste of their own medicine.' We remembered our own St. Paul's Cathedral 'standing among the ruins' and the agony and destruction inflicted on our city by the *Luftwaffe*. But, as we listened to the roar of the mighty fleets of Allied bombers flying over London to maintain the incessant bombing of German cities on a scale we had never known, we also remembered our own fear and trepidation as the German bombers approached throughout that punishing winter of 1940–1. Some found it in their hearts to spare a thought for the German civilians who, that night, would face the terror we had so long endured.

An air of listlessness began to appear on the face of my drivers and others in the area. I guess the same might have been said about me, too. When my opposite number, Les Smith said, one day, 'What's up, Dee? You're not looking too good'; the thought flashed through my mind that he, also, was not looking too good. The strain was beginning to show, but I replied, 'Nothing that a good night's sleep won't cure.' And restful sleep, I suppose, was the greatest need of many of us at that stage of the war. I felt in my bones that the end was in sight but the natural exhilaration was overshadowed by the daily tragedies. After the war, one of our firewomen told me that as she contemplated the end of hostilities, there was the fear in her mind that she might be one of those unfortunates to die as the result of one of the last rockets to strike. That thought had crossed my mind and, I am sure, that of many others. Morbid? Perhaps. We had all lived in the Shadow so long that we realised that, but for the Grace of God, our names, too, would have appeared on the List of Civilian War Casualties. We all hoped that our luck would hold.

March dragged towards its close. On the 26th there were nine rocket incidents; on the 27th, six. At a few minutes before 1700 hours what we now know was to be the last rocket to explode on British soil landed at Orpington in Kent. From then on, there was an uneasy peace. The lull continued until the end of the month; the next day was 1 April, All Fool's Day. Would this bring a flood of rockets? Has Jerry been saving up for a final volley of death? It was the sort of devilish thinking that he had demonstrated on past occasions. But, as one peaceful day succeeded another, spirits revived and confidence grew.

My drivers greeted me, 'Good morning, sir, lovely day,' and singing could be heard coming from the women's quarters. A few unbroken night's sleep and freedom from explosion had lifted the tension and there were smiles again in the Control Rooms.

On April 12 came news of the death of President Franklin D. Roosevelt, our great American friend and Ally. This, from the Allied point of view, was the only cloud on the horizon. News of the surrender of enemy strongholds in Germany and Italy came so fast that it was difficult to find newspaper space to report them.

The Italian Dictator, Mussolini, was captured by a group of Italian partisans on 28 April in a village in Northern Italy. He was tried, sentenced to death and executed, together with members of his cabinet and his mistress, Clara Petacchi. Their bodies were taken to Milan and hung by the feet in a city square.

On 29 April, the German Forces fighting in Italy surrendered unconditionally. On May 3 the British Fourteenth Army liberated the port of Rangoon, thus virtually ending the long Burma Campaign. Next day, Field Marshal Montgomery received a delegation of Senior German Army Officers who agreed to the unconditional surrender of all the German Forces in Holland, Belgium and northwest Germany. On May 8 Prime Minister Winston Churchill broadcast news of the surrender of all the German Forces.

The war in Europe, at long last, was over.

That night the whole country erupted in a frenzy of joy. Great crowds gathered in Whitehall and in front of a floodlit Buckingham Palace, there to cheer the Royal Family; Winston Churchill and

members of the Cabinet. Every street in London seemed to have its
bonfire, some several. Bombed premises were stripped of anything
combustible and some quite dangerous situations arose when bonfires
were laid on wooden-block surfaced roads or built too close to
timber fences or other hazards, necessitating the attendance of the
fire service. In the Controls, firewomen were kept busy mobilising
appliances and chalking up the addresses of unattended calls, so
reminiscent of the blitz days and nights. The off duty girls, no doubt,
went out into the streets to join in the singing and dancing.

I went up to the roof of Cannon Street Fire Station and looked
out over a London lit by the glare of thousands of bonfires, with
clouds of golden sparks and smoke billowing about; a most authentic
reproduction of the night of the City Blitz. The only thing missing
was the drone of German bombers overhead.

The Dome of St. Paul's, towering in the light of four searchlight
beams shining on the Golden Cross, projected a great shadow of
the Cross on the clouds, high above. Firemen came in for a rough
time from the crowds when they judged a bonfire dangerous and
gave it a dousing. It was a marvellous night to let off steam; the
dancing and singing lasted until dawn when most of the revellers
had had enough and made their weary way homewards.

The next day, May 9 had been declared a public holiday when
the lively scenes of the previous day were repeated. It was also the
day when a Thanksgiving Service, attended by the Royal Family,
members of the Cabinet and Service Chiefs, was held in St. Paul's
Cathedral.

Many local boroughs held their own Thanksgiving Service in
churches and open spaces. The Fire Service could be relied upon
to provide a good turn out and local units were regularly invited to
take part. Firewoman Irene Wood, attached to Fulham Fire Station,
recalls the victory Parade and Divine Service in Bishops's Park.

'We had a little dog called Red. He was a rover and ran away at intervals but he always returned. On one occasion he was away for two weeks before recognising our pump which was attending a fire in Kensington. When the lads returned to the machine, there was Red sitting in the driver's seat. He had chosen the Red Watch and that's how he got his name.

'On the morning of the parade, I was given the job of leading Red in the march. We gave him a bath the night before and a good brush down. He was looking very smart, trotting along in front of the firewomen with a big red bow on his collar and behaved himself very well all the way to the park. Our detachment received a warm welcome from the large crowds and Red came in for a special ovation.

'But it was a different story in the park. We were positioned a few yards from a clump of trees and I spent the whole of the duration of the Service tugging on the lead to keep the little wretch away from those trees, much to the amusement of onlookers.'

In June 1945, many firewomen received preliminary notice of their forthcoming discharge from the Service. Approximately three months notice was given to enable the women to find other employment. A few Authorities had decided that there was a place for firewomen in the post-war service; other were welcomed back to the job they had left on call up but the majority faced discharge after, in many cases, six years of devoted service in a job they had come to love.

There were many expressions of appreciation from firewomen of their days spent as members of the Service.

'My proudest moments were spent in a wonderful Service, meeting and working with some very special people. I look back on those times as some of the best I ever spent.'

'I must say that wherever I worked the sense of camaraderie was wonderful. I have some splendid memories of people and incidents connected with the Fire Service and look back on the good times;

H. M. King George VI chats to firewomen on Stand Down Parade
in Hyde Park, 10 June 1945.

the friendships and the work we did during the war with great affection.'

'I was really happy as a firewoman; I had a satisfying job, one which only a wartime situation could provide. I made the most of it and, thought I say it myself, I gave of my best.'

'During the blitz the comradeship was unforgettable. Laughter kept us going and I have many wonderful memories of so many ordinary people doing impossible things. I am proud that I was there.'

'I must say I enjoyed it all. It seems a terrible thing to say, with all that death and destruction about, but my time in the National Fire Service were the best days of my life.'

And there were many more.

Firewomen lead the parade in the march past the King and Queen and the
Princess Elizabeth in Hyde Park, 10 June 1945.

I have endeavoured to cover in this book every aspect of a firewoman's work and to include stories from all the heavily bombed
cities. I tried to find firewomen from Bath and Canterbury with stories
to tell of the Baedeker Raids on those cities and others: from Clyde-
bank, Merseyside and the western and other ports, all of which experienced some of the most ferocious bombing of the war. Unfortunately,
they were not forthcoming. Nevertheless, if any ladies from these areas
read this story, I am sure they will recognise their own experiences in
the tales I have included from other parts of the country.

I started off a reluctant author, for no other reason than that
I thought the story of our wartime firewomen would come better
from a woman than a man, but certain of my former colleagues, ladies
who had served in the AFS and National Fire Service, pushed me

into it. I am now delighted that I took it on, for the tales I have been told have served only to increase my great admiration for the magnificent loyalty and pride of service demonstrated by Our Girls.

I have left this masterpiece of understatement to the last, for it epitomises so many of the stories submitted by firewomen in a self-effacing, almost apologetic manner. It is Firewoman Elsie Maskell's story and I have reproduced it almost precisely as she wrote:

I joined the Fire Service part time in 1938 at Station 22, Burdett Road for one night a week to learn all about the fire alarm system and where they were situated. On September 1 1939, I was called in to my boss's office where he told me he had had a phone call from Burdett Road to tell me I was to report at once with my car (a Morris Cowley) to my station.

I spent about twelve months there between Coborn Road and Southern Grove School driving a light van to several stations with hoses, etc.

When the blitz started I was kept busy driving a canteen to the City of London to the firemen fighting the fires. Then I would return to my station and take out the light van with 2 gallon petrol cans to the fires in the city for the appliances, as they were getting low on petrol. This happened several times while the blitz was on.

After a time, I was sent to Homerton to drive a Mobile Kitchen with two cooks and we went out daily to different sub-stations while their kitchens were being decorated. We had a quiet spell and the two cooks and I took part in the trailer pump competition at Lambeth HQ.

One night, the kitchen was ordered to go to Norwich with a convoy of fire appliances to help with the fire burning there and we went to feed the men. The kitchen carried 100 gallons of water, 5 cwt. of coal and knives, forks and spoons for 200 firemen. The stove was like a ship's galley, the baking tins of batter pudding cut up to forty portions.

I was then sent to Manor Road school, West Ham with the kitchen

and when not required, took over a petrol tanker and helped out
the men at the stations. When the sirens went, I drove the tanker
to an open piece of land nearby in case of accident and collected it
after the 'all clear'.

Then we were all moved out to Abbey Road School, West Ham,
as they wanted to re-open Manor Road School. I had a slight
accident to my foot and was taken to hospital. When I returned, I
found the school had been hit by a doodlebug; two of our firemen
had been killed and a number injured. I was at Abbey Road throughout the main doodlebug attack until September 1944.

I was on the move again to Woodford Bridge Training School
when the V2 attack was at its height and, finally, was sent to Ley
Street Control to drive the Control Van as required.

I was demobbed in 1945 and returned to my old printing firm
after six years as a firewoman.

People with experience of the blitz will not find it hard to visualise
what Elsie has failed to mention in her account; the times, the many
times when she was terrified and shocked by her exposure to bombing;
her narrow escapes and news of the violent death of close friends and
colleagues, at times within her sight. The periods of tension, when
she had to summon up every ounce of courage, strength and perseverance she possessed to complete the task she had been given.

Elsie's duties, like those of her colleagues up and down the country,
demanded a high degree of initiative, courage and devotion to duty,
often in the face of great danger and frequently without supervision.
When she drove her petrol tanker through a hail of red hot shrapnel
from anti-aircraft gun-fire and the threat of bomb splinters, to park
it safely away from the station yard 'in case of accident', she did so
at the risk of a horrible death. But there was no mention of that in
her story, although I am quite sure it was in the forefront of her
mind at the time.

Epilogue

THE heaviest and most devastating air raid of the war took place on the night of May 10–11 1940, when 500 bombers dropped some 700 tonnes of incendiary and high explosive bombs on London. Fifteen hundred civilians were killed, thirty-five of them firemen, on that terrible night.

Now, fifty years later almost to the day, a Memorial to those members of the Fire Service who died by enemy action was to be unveiled by Her Majesty Queen Elizabeth the Queen Mother in Old Change Court, just across the way from the Cathedral, where so many firemen had battled to drive back the flames that threatened to destroy St. Paul's itself.

The Unveiling was preceded by a Service of Remembrance in St. Paul's in the presence of Her Majesty. The next of kin of those who perished and veterans who served in the AFS and National Fire Service filled every seat, wearing their Honours and Medals with pride. They came, from Caithness to Cornwall, to pay homage to over 1,000 members of the Service who answered a call from which they failed to return.

The atmosphere in the Cathedral was emotional. Many handkerchiefs were seen, somewhat furtively dabbing eyes during the singing of the hymn 'Abide with me'. The pain of parting has eased in the half century since the dark days, but memories of loved ones were still fresh among members of that great congregation.

After the Service, clergy and congregation walked across the road to where the Memorial stood shrouded in the Union Jack, standing

Her Majesty, Queen Elizabeth the Queen mother, unveils the Memorial,
watched by the Chief Fire Officer, London, and staff officers.
The Dean of St Paul's Cathedral begins the Dedication.

The names of firewomen killed by enemy action are commemorated on this panel at the base of the Fire Service Memorial. A staff car driver and a despatch rider flank the tablet bearing the names of the fallen.

in the sunshine of a lovely May morning. After a short address, Her Majesty unveiled the Memorial which the Very Reverend Dean of St. Paul's Dedicated in these words: 'In the faith of Jesus Christ we dedicate this Memorial to the Glory of God, and in memory of these his servants who gave their lives in the service of their country and the defence of their homeland, in the name of the Father, and of the Son and of the Holy Ghost. Amen.'

The Queen Mother delighted the large crowd surrounding the Memorial by 'going walkabout' and speaking to many of them. Following her departure, there was a surge of people searching the panels for the name of a loved one; many were moved to tears as they found what they were seeking.

Mrs Doris Farris, who joined the AFS in 1938 and who served in the London Region throughout the war, was among those present. There were many reunions of old comrades, some of whom last met nearly half a century ago. Doris met up with four from her Bethnal Green days. As they stood chatting, Doris pointed to a name on a panel and remarked to her friends 'That's one of our pump's crew that was wiped out on 10 September 1940.' A woman standing next to her, a complete stranger, grasped her hand and cried 'That's my dad. Did you know him? Tell me about him.' She was so pleased and excited to meet someone who had known her father. After a few moments conversation she told Doris 'I was only three when he died.'

The Firewomen's panel at the base attracted considerable interest. It portrays a staff car driver and a despatch rider flanking the list of names of firewomen who died by enemy action.

Many difficulties had to be overcome in making the project feasible. The planners suffered several disappointments and setbacks over the years in their efforts to erect a permanent Memorial to the men and women of the Fire Service who died tin the battle against the bombers. It is sad that many old comrades who had hoped to see their mates publicly commemorated have, themselves, passed on. But those of us who survive will look on the Memorial with pride and quiet satisfaction and, perhaps, stroll across the road for a few moments of prayer and reflection in the Cathedral that so many firemen battled to preserve.

Addendum

MANY countries throughout the world, notably the United States, have a long history of women firefighters. In Great Britain, however, women were not considered for employment as firefighters before 1982, when the London Fire Brigade resolved to admit women to it's operational force.

It cannot be said that there has been a great surge of women recruits, anxious to take advantage of the opportunity of embarking on a career as a firefighter, for, thirteen years later, there are only sixty women serving whole-time as firefighters in the London Fire Brigade, representing less than one per cent of the brigade's operational strength. A further six women are in training and some twenty are employed in provincial fire brigades.

The pay and conditions of service, like the entrance examination, are the same for both sexes. On applying to join the London Fire Brigade, the candidate must satisfy the examiner that he or she is at least five feet six inches tall, There is an upper height limit of six feet four inches, although this condition is unlikely to disqualify many women applicants! The candidate must also pass an educational and a strength test. A simple machine registers the power of the candidate's grip, using each hand. The strength of the legs and back is measured by a machine which is adjusted to the individual's height; he or she must exceed a minimum reading on the dial to pass the test.

The aerobic test consists of stepping up and down at a steady rate on a platform about one foot high. This test lasts five minutes, after which the pulse rate is checked and other tests made. The medical

Leading Firefighter (now Station Officer) Sian Griffiths, wearing breathing apparatus, after an hour's hard labour in a heavily smoked basement at a four pump fire at Clerkenwell, London.

examination is searching, as it must be for entry to a profession that is so physically demanding. Having overcome all these barriers, the recruit will receive a letter informing him or her of the conditions of employment as a firefighter and stating the date for the commencement of training.

Standard training is carried out at the Brigade Training Centre at Southwark Bridge Road. Upon reporting on the opening day of the Course, the recruit is issued with all necessary uniform; the women are issued with the same firefighting gear as the men. The only difference in the uniform issue is that operational women are permitted, out of choice, to wear trousered undress uniform although all are issued with a uniform skirt.

Viewing a mixed crew at exercise in the drill yard, I found it impossible to tell whether I was watching a man or a woman. I devised my own method of identification; I observed the size of the feet and, generally, it was accurate. Using this method, I picked as a woman, correctly, the operator at the head of the turntable ladder and the individual holding the branch at pump drill.

The duration of the initial training course is twenty weeks which includes two weeks special training in the use of breathing apparatus. Recruits are also required to face up to realistic practise fires, designed to provide experience of working in smoke and the heat punishment and restricted vision they will be exposed to at an actual outbreak. Here they will gain their first experience of the severe physical demands the business of firefighting imposes on the human frame. They will emerge from their first encounter with raging fire exhausted, perspiring freely, tingling with excitement and with the adrenalin in full flow. And, if made of the right stuff, they will be keenly anticipating their first real 'job'.

The modern fire brigade is frequently called upon to provide what it terms 'Special Service'. Train and aircraft crashes; road traffic accidents; people trapped in machinery and lifts, would-be suicides under tube trains and a host of other sometimes bizarre situations involving human beings and, occasionally, animals in peril. Brigade appliances carry a varied assortment of tools to deal with these emergencies and the recruit receives training in the use of this often complicated hydraulic or electrically powered equipment.

I was given the opportunity of speaking to a few experienced women firefighters. Remembering my own initial confrontation with a gruesome 'man under a bus' incident, when I felt physically sick and had literally to force myself to 'get down and under', I asked one of the women what her reaction was to a gory RTA (road traffic accident). 'It doesn't worry me at all' was her reply. 'I just carry on doing what I have to do and disregard the rest.' Others I

After all the training, this is the real thing.
Firefighters recover the remains of some unfortunate from under a tube train at
East Ham. Firefighter Jacqueline Le Fevre, right, up at the sharp end with her
crew mates.

spoke to admitted that they do not relish attending this type of special service but agreed that it is an essential part of the job that has to be accepted in the course of duty. When I asked 'What is your general attitude to the job', all, in effect, answered 'I love it. Every minute of it. I cannot imagine myself doing anything else.'

Firefighting, clearly, is not every woman's, or, for that matter, every man's cup of tea, but it is an attractive occupation to those who have the inclination and the attributes. Those London women firefighters who have accepted the challenge, taking on what for many years has been considered essentially a man's job, have demonstrated their ability to maintain, at least, the standards set by the brigade.

Those I spoke to mentioned a degree of resentment against women firefighters held by a small number of their male colleagues. The majority are without prejudice and it is my guess that 'the few' will come to appreciate the value of their women colleagues as did those doubters in the immediate pre-blitz days. I was told by one of the male training officers that, in the early days, the novelty of working beside a woman firefighter often led to a protective attitude on the part of the fireman. 'Leave that to me' was common advice to a woman when a heavy or unpleasant job came along. That attitude quickly evaporated when it was realised that women not only were prepared to take on any task but were quite capable of sharing the burden equally.

There was consensus among the women that they need regular physical exercise to maintain and increase their bodily strength. Much of their need is met by the routine fire exercises at station level, using the heavy brigade equipment originally designed for use exclusively by male personnel. The Service requires it's firefighters to maintain a high level of physical fitness. Routine drills and exercises and, of course, the daily quota of operational action, play their part in achieving a generally good standard. As an extra measure, each fire station had a well equipped gymnasium where firefighters may cycle, skip, jog and, in some cases row, to their heart's content, service commitments allowing. Sport is encouraged in the Brigade and women firefighters have a wide range of interests, among them swimming, cycling, sailing, volley ball, athletics, rock climbing and jogging.

All those I spoke to expressed an interest in advancement in the Brigade. Several have passed the examination for leading firefighter, sub-officer and one had qualified for promotion to station officer rank. Judging from the number of A and O levels of education held by the women, there will be more to come.

REST IN PEACE

ASHCROFT, RHODA

BAKER, LILIAN

BARTLETT, JOAN

CARRINGTON, DOROTHY

CHITTY, PEARL

DAVIES, MARJORIE

DAY, HILDA

DUNCAN, DOREEN

DUPREE, HILDA

GIFFORD, ALICE

HALL, HILDA

HAWTIN, ELSIE

HOWARD, RUBY

HUXLEY, FRANCES

KERLEY, DAISY

LAY, DORIS

LONG, BEATRICE

MILLER, JOSEPHINE

PENGELLY, VIOLET

PETERS, WINIFRED

PICKETT, QUEENIE

KIDD, JOAN

YOUNG, SYBIL

Index